9th Workshop on Constraint Grammar and Finite State NLP - Rule-based and hybrid methods and tools for user communities (CG/FST-NLP 2025)

Tallinn, Estonia
5 March 2025

ISBN: 979-8-3313-1885-7

Printed from e-media with permission by:

Curran Associates, Inc.
57 Morehouse Lane
Red Hook, NY 12571

Some format issues inherent in the e-media version may also appear in this print version.

Printed with permission by Curran Associates, Inc. (2025)

For permission requests, please contact the Association for Computational Linguistics at the address below.

Association for Computational Linguistics
209 N. Eighth Street
Stroudsburg, Pennsylvania 18360

Phone: 1-570-476-8006
Fax: 1-570-476-0860

acl@aclweb.org

Additional copies of this publication are available from:

Curran Associates, Inc.
57 Morehouse Lane
Red Hook, NY 12571 USA
Phone: 845-758-0400
Fax: 845-758-2633
Email: curran@proceedings.com
Web: www.proceedings.com

CG/FST-NLP 2025

The 9th Workshop on Constraint Grammar and Finite State NLP – Rule-based and hybrid methods and tools for user communities

Proceedings of the Workshop

March 5, 2025

Introduction

We are delighted to invite you to CG-FST NLP 2025, the ninth NoDaLiDa workshop on Constraint Grammar (CG). Constraint grammars often take text analysed with the help of finite state transducers (FST), which is why we have also invited papers on FST this year. The conference is being held as a physical event only, on March 5th 2025, at the NoDaLiDa conference in Tallinn.

Constraint Grammar is a grammar formalism developed in the Nordic countries. The main open source implementation FSTs, Helsinki finite state transducer, or HFST, was made in Finland. It is thus only to be expected that this workshop series is a pendant to NoDaLiDa/Baltic-HLT. The first CG workshop was arranged at NoDaLiDa in Odense in 2009, and it has been arranged at every NoDaLiDa conference ever since, except for at the 23rd NoDaLiDa in Reykjavik in 2021 (which was held mostly as a virtual event, due to the COVID pandemic).

Topic-wise, the papers in this year's workshop may be divided into three groups: Five of the papers deal mainly with one language, and present a spellchecker (Horváth, Rueter and Trosterud), grammar checker (Bick; Denbæk) or grammatical analysis (Gerstenberger; Trosterud and Vonen). Four of the papers take a more general approach, and deal with the functionalities of Constraint grammar (Swanson; Wiechetek and Unhammer) or FST (Pirinen and Moshagen) as proofing tools. Finally, one paper (Torstensson and Holmström) is a hybrid paper investigating the role of (possibly CG) annotated data may play for LLMs. This year's workshop covers, not only a wide range of applications, but also different languages (Esperanto, Romanian, Mansi, Tokelau, Greenlandic, Lule Sámi, Irish).

We would like to thank the members of the program committee (Eckhard Bick, Tino Didriksen, Kaili Müürisep, Daniel Glen Swanson and Francis Tyers) for taking part in planning and organising the workshop. We would also like to thank the anonymous reviewers for reviewing the incoming papers. Without anonymous reviews there are no peer-reviewed proceedings, and their work is thus highly appreciated.

Trond Trosterud, General Chair

Linda Wiechetek and Flammie Pirinen, Program Co-Chairs

Organizing Committee

General Chair

Trond Trosterud, UiT The Arctic University of Norway

Program Chairs

Linda Wiechetek, UiT The Arctic University of Norway
Flammie Pirinen, UiT The Arctic University of Norway

Program Committee

Program Chairs

Eckhard Bick, University of Southern Denmark - SDU
Tino Didriksen, Oqaasileriffik
Kaili Müürisep, institute of computer science, University of Tartu
Flammie A Pirinen, Norgga árktalaš universitehta
Daniel Glen Swanson, Indiana University
Trond Trosterud, University of Tromsø
Francis M. Tyers, Indiana University, Bloomington
Linda Wiechetek, University of Tromsø

Reviewers

Eckhard Bick, University of Southern Denmark - SDU
Tino Didriksen, Oqaasileriffik
Kimmo Koskenniemi, University of Helsinki
Inari Listenmaa, Chalmers University of Technology
Kaili Müürisep, institute of computer science, University of Tartu
Marja-Liisa Olthuis
Flammie A Pirinen, Norgga árktalaš universitehta
Daniel Glen Swanson, Indiana University
Trond Trosterud, University of Tromsø
Francis M. Tyers, Indiana University, Bloomington
Kevin Brubeck Unhammer, Trigram
Linda Wiechetek, University of Tromsø

Table of Contents

Program

Wednesday, March 5, 2025

08:30 - 08:45	*Opening Remarks*
09:30 - 11:30	*Oral Session 1*
11:00 - 12:00	*Break*
12:00 - 14:00	*Oral Session 2*
14:00 - 15:00	*Break*
15:00 - 16:00	*Oral Session 3*

Wednesday, March 5, 2025 (continued)

16:00 - 17:00 *Panel Discussions and Business Meetings*

An Annotated Error Corpus for Esperanto

Eckhard Bick
University of Southern Denmark & GrammarSoft ApS
eckhard.bick@gmail.com

Abstract

This paper presents and evaluates a new multi-genre error corpus for (written) Esperanto, *EspEraro*, building on both learner, news and internet data and covering both ordinary spelling errors and real-word errors such as grammatical and word choice errors. Because the corpus has been annotated not onlyse for errors, error types and corrections, but also with Constraint Grammar (CG) tags for part-of-speech, inflection, affixation, syntactic function, dependency and semantic class, it allows users to linguistically contextualize errors and to craft and test CG rules aiming at the recognition and/or correction of the various error types covered in the corpus. The resource was originally created for regression-testing a newly developed spell- and grammar checker, and contains about 75,000 tokens (~ 4,000 sentences), with 3,330 tokens annotated for one or more errors and a combined correction suggestion. We discuss the different error types and evaluate their weight in the corpus. Where relevant, we explain the role of Constraint Grammar (CG) in the identification and correction of the individual error types.

1 Introduction

Error corpora have the potential to play an important role in modern linguistics, and can support diverse tasks such as pedagogical-didactic work, the development of spell- and grammar checkers, as well as research on language change and variation. Most of these corpora, however, are error corpora in the specialized sense that they contain L2 learner data covering one or more L1 languages, e.g. (Al-Jarf, 2010) with an overview for English, (Rakhilina et al., 2016) for Russian, or (Arnardóttir et al., 2022) for Icelandic.

Gamon et al. (2013) stress the three-fold importance of such corpora for automatic systems: error statistics, ML training and evaluation. However, it remains unclear how well L2 data carry over to native speaker errors. In addition, many of the available L2 resources are limited by the fact that they do not provide an actual error mark-up, let alone systematic error classification. The European CLARIN initiative[1], for instance, offers 75 learner corpora covering 15 languages. Yet only seven of these corpora are listed as providing actual error labels[2]. Also, and not least in a world-wide perspective, English is by far the best-represented L2, followed by a few dozen major and European languages at most, and no data at all for the vast majority of languages. Thus, in a global overview of learner corpora at the University of Louvain-la-Neuve[3], out of 208 corpora, 50% have English as the target language, followed by Spanish, German and Italian with 9% each, French (6%), Chinese, Russian (2%) and Arabic (1%).

An example of an error corpus that is *not* a learner corpus is Sketch Engine's *Error Corpus from English Wikipedia,* with seven error types (spelling, lexico-semantic, typos relating to style, punctuation, typographical, other). However, error tagging is unrevised, automatic only and mostly focuses on safe typographical errors[4], not mentioning grammatical errors. An interesting alternative, providing no error classification, but at least a corpus of manual corrections, is to export edit histories from Wikipedia (or other sources), a method suggested by Lichtarte et al. (2019) to procure training data for the automatic

[1] https://www.clarin.eu/resource-families/L2-corpora
[2] for English, Czech, Norwegian, Slovene, Hungarian, Spanish, German/Italian
[3] https://uclouvain.be/en/research-institutes/ilc/cecl/learner-corpora-around-the-world.html
[4] https://www.sketchengine.eu/error-corpus-from-english-wikipedia/

Proceedings of the 9th Workshop on Constraint Grammar and Finite State NLP, pages 1–8

correction of grammatical errors. On a general note, shared task training data is a valuable source of structured and comparable corpus data in the ML community, and the upcoming *Shared task on Multilingual Grammatical Error Correction* at the 2025 NLP4CALL workshop[5] will involve sentence correction pairs for at least 10 languages, albeit without error classification proper.

EspEraro, the Esperanto corpus presented here - to the best or our knowledge the first of its kind - is intended to fill a data gap for this under-resourced language, providing a wide scope of errors, with all data fully analyzed at various linguistic levels. Unlike many other error/learner corpora, EspEraro provides not just learner data or other error-containing material, but points out where and what the errors are, with a fine-grained error classification system for real-word errors, and manual revision for all mark-up.

2 The corpus

EspEraro contains about 4,400 Constraint Grammar-annotated sentences with 75,000 tokens, of which 3,330 are marked for one or more error types, as well as a combined correction suggestion. The CG tags used adhere to the cross-language VISL convention (Bick 2023). The corpus was developed as part of an ongoing spell- and grammar checker project Lingvohelpilo-2[6], in which it was used for regression testing[7], and the inclusion of error types and sentences in the corpus was often motivated by challenges encountered during development. Therefore, in addition to presenting the various error types and evaluating their relative impact on the corpus (section 3), we will also discuss the methods that were used to identify and correct them, with a special focus on the role of Constraint Grammar, explaining some of the about 2,000 rules used in the Lingvohelpilo-2 project.

Corpus material was added from three different sources, reflecting different phases of development:

(a) learner sentences from the online teaching portal Lernu![8], containing a non-systematic variety of errors both orthographical and grammatical

(b) text book error examples from various sources and modified dictionary quotes[9], systematically covering grammatical errors and certain particles

(c) corpus sentences containing lexical errors (word choice, false friends, confusable word pairs), plus random errors co-occurring with the former.

Type (c) material constitutes the main part of the collection and was harvested from a 200 million word reference corpus of news, literature, wikipedia and a variety of internet sources, hoping to capture not just learner errors, but a representative cross section of frequent errors made by the language community as a whole. In this sense, the corpus transcends what is normally understood as an L2 corpus. However, the roots of Esperanto are artificial, and the language is not linked to any regionally defined political entity, nation or ethnic group, and with the notable exception of mixed-marriage native speaker children, most language users are therefore L2 speakers. Given the language's regular grammar and affixation system, the learning period proper will be considerably shorter than for other languages, but even fluent speakers may still make errors, not least caused by L1 interference or first foreign language interference (often English). In addition, due to the lack of a dominant native speaker community, there is a high tolerance for lexical and syntactic variation, exerting less pressure on the individual to become aware of and avoid interference errors. Because of these factors, the borders between a learner-error corpus, an L2 corpus and a wider error corpus for "native" speakers is blurred in the case of Esperanto.

The reference corpus is available for searching and statistical analysis in the CorpusEye interface (https://corp.visl.dk), and contains morphosyntactic, dependency and semantic annotation provided by the EspGram Constraint Grammar parser (Bick 2007). We used this corpus in a dual fashion. First, to identify frequent orthographical errors and error patterns,

[5] https://spraakbanken.gu.se/en/research/themes/icall/nlp4call-workshop-series/nlp4call2025
[6] https://lingvohelpilo.visl.dk/, with financial support from ESF (Esperantic Studies Foundation)
[7] This is why the corpus also contains a certain amount of error-free sentences, covering cases where false positive markings where addressed. For the same reason, sentences are not contiguous, but collected.
[8] https://lernu.net
[9] The main dictionary sources were ReVo (https://reta-vortaro.de) and PIV (Plena Ilustrita Vortaro, http://vortaro.net

we ran statistics on lower-case words marked as heuristic or compounded and frequency-sorted the result for inspection and automatic look-up of their lemmas[10]. Obviously, the method also throws up foreign words, neologisms and unrecognized derivations, but it did help to identify frequent error patterns, e.g. confusion of consonant or vowel pairs, or jumbled consonant clusters, as well as OCR artifact error patterns (e.g. 'm' vs. 'rn' [r+n]) and Esperanto-specific encoding confusion issues with diacritics (e.g. '¸' = ĝ, 'ÿ' = ŝ, '∑' = Ŝ , 'u˘' = ŭ etc.).

Second, we used the corpus to find usage examples of grammatical errors, for instance agreement clashes in NP's (number or case) or between subject and subject predicative (number). We also checked for transitivity errors by doing dependency searches for intransitive verbs having direct objects, or looking for passive participles of intransitive verbs. Esperanto does not allow dual transitivity usage and uses affixed to make intransitive verbs transitive or vice versa, so the method will flag either usage errors or affixation errors. Finally, we used the reference corpus to look up false friends or word confusion pairs suggested in the literature, identifying grammatical and lexical trigger contexts for the mapping rules marking the confusion error in question. At the same time, one or more typical error usage cases, and sometimes a correct counter example, would go into the EspEraro corpus for regression testing.

3 Error types

Currently, the error corpus contains 3860 individual instances of error type markings[11] attached to 3330 "annotation tokens"[12]. The error markings come in three variants, depending on the marking method used in the proofing tool. Non-word errors that are similar to an existing word xxx (a) are marked with the latter in the form of an <R:xxx> correction tag and a <W:[0-9]+> Levenshtein similarity value[13]. Errors found through lexical lookup and pattern-recognition (b) are classified as <E-TYPE:....>, and CG-mapped error types (c) use a CG-recognizable prefix (@....). Correction suggestions <R:...> for (b) and (c) are either generated on-the-fly in conjunction with error-classification, or post-generated based on corrected POS and inflection tags.

The CG-annotated example sentence in figure 1 contains — marked in red — a non-word *(konfrmis),* a lemma substitution error *(perfortigita),* two accusative case errors *(morganata[n] geedzeco[n]),* one transitivity error *(translokis)* and an article insertion *(la).* Depending on how the sentence is interpreted, there could also be a subclause-end comma before *'kaj'* (marked on the latter as *@comma-FSend).* Note that the annotation retains, in addition to the error tagging, all relevant VISL CG tag fields:

Word [lemma] <secondary> POS MORPH &syntax #dependency

with <secondary> containing tags for subclass (e.g. <rel> relative pronoun, <fem> = female, <mv> = main verb), valency (e.g. <vt> = transitive verb), semantic prototype (e.g. <Hprof> = human professional, <Ltown>), framenet (e.g. <fn:hurt>), sentiment (<Q+/->), derivation/compounding (e.g. <F:ge%edz%ec|o>) and coordination structure (e.g. <cjt-first>).

Ŝi [ŝi] <fem> PERS 3S F NOM &SUBJ> #1->2 *She*

anoncis [anonci] <vq> <fn:declare> <mv> V IMPF VFIN &FS-STA #2->0 *declared*

, [,] PU #3->2

ke [ke] KS &SUB #4->6 *that*

ŝi [ŝi] <fem> PERS 3S F NOM &SUBJ> #5->7 *she*

estis [esti] <aux> <cjt-first> V IMPF VFIN &FS-<ACC #6->2 *was*

perfortigita [devigi] **<R:devigita>** <fn:be_attribute> <Q-> <fn:hurt> <PRP:per+fort%ig|i> <mv> V PCP PAS IMPF ADJ S NOM &ICL-AUX< &ICL-AUX< @:BASE-devigi #7->6 *forced*

rezigni [rezigni] <fn:refrain> <Q-> <mv> V INF &ICL-<SA #8->7 *to resign*

kaj [kaj] <clb> KC &CO #9->6 *and*

translokis [transloki] **<R:translokiĝis>** <cjt> <PRP:trans+lok|i> <fn:transfer> <mv> V IMPF VFIN &FS-STA @iĝ #10->2 *moved*

al [al] PRP &<OA #11->10 *to*

Romo [Romo] <Ltown> PROP S NOM &P< #12->11

, [,] PU #13->12 *Rome*

kie [kie] <rel><aloc> ADV &ADVL> #14->21 *where*

[10] In Esperanto, lemmatization is not in itself an error source, because after filtering of a few function words, word class and inflection can be safely predicted from endings.

[11] not counting the secondary tag of "green" (not a serious error, or not regarded as an error by some).

[12] An annotation token may not necessarily be space-delimited. Thus, multi-part named entities are regarded as one token, and for word splitting and word fusion may be annotated together as one token. Also, word insertions are counted as tokens.

[13] Computed based on editing distance, phonetic similarity, keyboard likelihood and frequency.

la [la] ART @insert #15->15 *the*

tiama [tiama] <jtime> ADJ S NOM &>N #16->17 *then pope Gregory the 16th*

papo [papo] <Hprof> N S NOM &SUBJ> #17->21

Gregorio [Gregorio] PROP S NOM &N< #18->17

la [la] ART &>N #19->20

16-a [16-a] <num-ord> ADJ S NOM &N< #20->18

konfrmis [konfirmi] <vq> <fn:confirm> **<R:konfirmis>** <W:2124> <mv> V IMPF VFIN &FS-N< #21->12 *confirmed*

ŝian [ŝia] <fem> <poss> DET S ACC &>N #22->24 *her*

morganata [morganata] **<R:morganatan>** ADJ S ACC &>N @acc #23->24 *morganatic*

geedzeco [geedzeco] **<R:geedzecon>** <F:ge%edz %ec|o> <f-soc> N S ACC &<ACC @acc #24->21

. [.] PU #25->2 *marriage*

Figure 1: Annotated sentence

About 15.7% of all errors are examples of purely orthographical errors, or 13.3% if casing errors are excluded. About 40% of these[14] are similarity-based corrections of unrecognized words. In addition to Levenshtein similarity weighting (cf. <W:[0-9]+> tags), we rely on the ordinary CG disambiguation rules of the EspGram parser to weed out contextually unfit correction suggestions. Another 40% of the simple spelling errors are identified using a special dictionary of orthographical error patterns and deprecated word forms. The remainder (20%) is handled by a mixture of (lexicon-informed) preprocessing and CG rules. The former handles encoding-based errors and some OCR errors, alongside the normalisation process for Esperanto diacritics[15]. It may also suggest word fusions or splittings that will then be validated using CG rules. The latter can also add word fusions themselves, based on "impossible" context such as same-case N-N chains. In addition, CG is used to mark and correct hyphenation errors and numbering format errors, e.g. dates, ordinal endings and decimal markers, as well as marking upper case / lower case errors. Here, SUBSTITUTE rules with unifications variables are used to suggest corrections, while ADD rules are used for error tags that leave the actual correction to an external generator (e.g. @upper, @lower):

```
(r1) SUBSTITUTE ("[^<]+"r)
("$1-$2"v <error> <E-TYPE:missing-hyphen>)
TARGET ("([A-Z][A-Z]+|[0-9]+)([a-z]+)"r <heur>)

(r2) ADD (@lower) TARGET <*>
(0 <jnat> OR ("[a-z]+e"r <PROP:.*\\|e>r ADV))
(-1 ALL-ORD - <*>)  (NOT 1 (<*>))
```

Rule (r1) marks and inserts a missing hyphen in words like *'UEA(-)delegito'* (UEA delegate) and *'3(-)ĉambra'* (3-bedroom). The simplified rule (r2) marks uppercase <*> nationality adjectives <jnat> and name- (PROP) derived adverbs (ADV) as lower case (@lower), unless they are sentence-initial or part of an uppercased MWE, i.e. with an upper-case word before or after.

The spellchecker offers the user a fine-grained choice of activating or inactivating individual error types, in order to avoid having to look at and ignore false positive markings. In the same vein, the tool marks dictionary-wise unknown names, compounds and derivations as such rather than throwing up an error[16]. Foreign words are much less safe to distinguish from spelling errors, so a tag is shown (@foreign, 2% of markings in the corpus). Words that are not likely to be either, and do not have a small edit distance to a known word, are marked as @new[17] (1.3% in the corpus). These may be true lexicon gaps, e.g. *traĥikarpo* (a tree), *ortparalele,* name-like nouns, e.g. *laolumoj, tuĝja-oj* (ethnic groups) or unrecognized, mostly Romance, foreign words, e.g. *protezione, geofisica, piranha.*

In terms of Constraint Grammar, real word-errors, i.e. grammatical and word choice errors, are the most relevant categories, because they can only be handled by including context and semantics. Thus, rule (r3), mapping a direction-accusative ending on place nouns (N-LOC) relies heavily on both valency (e.g. for adverbial arguments <va+DIR/LOC>,<vta+DIR/LOC>),

[14] i.e. of the 13.3%

[15] Depending on keyboard options, the circumflex in the letters ĉ, ĝ, ĥ, ĵ, ŝ and ŭ is sometimes replaced with an 'x' or an 'h'. Whereas the former is almost always uniquely reversible, the latter may create a small amount of ambiguity to be resolved.

[16] EspEraro retains the full morphological analysis, so there will be a POS tag for names (PROP) and a segmented analysis for compound parts and affixes for complex words.

[17] These may be foreign words that *look* like Esperanto words (e.g. *vulcanologia*), esperantized Chinese roots (e.g. *ĝingluo-o*) or triple-compound words (e.g. *hom+riĉ+font%an,* with + being a root boundary and % an affix boundary)

semantic prototypes (e.g. <Lpath>, <con> [container], <an.*> [anatomicals], <cc-h> [made things]) and a semantic verb set (V-MOVE-I [intransitive movement verbs]):

```
(r3) ADD (@acc-dir) TARGET N-LOC + NOM
(*-1 PRP-LOC BARRIER NON-PRE-N/ADV LINK NOT 0 ("trans") OR ("ĉe") OR ("ĉirkaux") LINK *-1 VV BARRIER NON-ADV OR <adir> LINK 0 <va+DIR> - V-MOVE-I - <ve> OR <vta+DIR> LINK NOT 0 <va+LOC> OR <vta+LOC>)
(NOT 0 <Lpath> OR <an.*>r)
((NEGATE 0 <con> OR (<cc-h>) LINK p ("en")) OR (*p ("meti") OR ("ŝuti") OR ("verŝi")))
```

With a narrow definition, leaving out word insertions, deletions and substitutions, there are about 35 grammatical error categories, covering POS, affixation and inflection errors, that amounts to 22.0% of all errors in the corpus.

Tag	Error	%
acc	accusative -n: object	31.6
acc-dir, acc-oc, -quant, -trans	accusative -n: other complements	14.1
nom, nom-oc, -pcp, -prp	nominative: all uses	15.6
refl, no-refl	reflexive pronoun	1.5
adj, adv, noun	POS errors	4.0
-io, -iu	correlative pronoun	0.9
pl	plural	8.9
sg	singular	3.8
akt, pas	active vs. passive	1.1
ata, ita	aspect	1.1
vfin, as, is, os	finity/tense	4.9
us, u	finity/non-tense	0.9
inf	infinitive	1.3
ig/iĝ (affixes)	missing (in)transitivity	5.9
DEL:ig/iĝ	spurious (in)transitivity	3.4
ado, ul	other affixes	0.9
		99.9

Table 1: Grammatical errors

As can be seen from table 1, Esperanto's only case inflection ending, the accusastive -n, accounts for almost half the errors (45.7%) when including both nominal (object/subject, argument of preposition), predicatives and andverbial functions (direction, quantity). Note that while the corpus consists of chosen examples and for the sake of coverage needs to over-represent small error classes, the high frequency of accusative errors is nevertheless indicative, if not representative, for the language as a whole, as these errors also co-occur as "by-catch" in many sentences chosen for the sake of other errors.

Number agreement errors (sg, pl) make up the second largest group (12.7%) followed by transitivity suffix (ig/iĝ) errors (10.2%) with 10.2% verb inflection errors (9.4%). As might be expected for categories where one alternative is unmarked, wrongly adding an inflection ending or suffix is less frequent than wrongly omitting it. Thus, using a plural ending is more "premeditated" and less likely to be wrong (sg) than forgetting it (pl), and using an explicit transitivity marker spuriously is less likely than simply using an intransitive verb root with an object or as a passive – a "false friend" usage that is seen in English, German and many other natural languages (e.g. *to begin, end, roll, run, open).*

A few grammatical error categories, while tagged on one individual token, have a wider scope and imply changes in more than one token, in which case no <R:...> correction tag can be shown. Thus, the lack of a subject is marked on the finite verb (@PREADD:subject), 3.2%) and inverted order is marked on the second word (@PRESWAP, 1.4%). Finally, a @warning tag (0.6%) is used on tokens with a syntactically impossible context, but no simple/local correction. Finding this type of error is a CG task. (r4), for instance, throws a warning for finite verbs (VFIN) directly following left-attaching subjects (&<SUBJ) without a left context of a clause-boundary word (CLB-ORD) or a right-attaching sister subject (sl &SUBJ>):

```
(r4) ADD (@warning) TARGET VFIN
(-1C &<SUBJ LINK *-1 VFIN LINK NEGATE *-1 CLB-ORD)
(NEGATE -1 &<SUBJ LINK sl &SUBJ>)
```

This rule calls for a 1-verb rephrasing of a sentence with two clashing verbs, likely originating from a copy-paste error:

Cetere *(by the way)*, la 23an de junio *(23 June)* **okazas** *(takes place)* la sporta mondo *(the sport world)* **celebras** *(celebrates)* ĉiujare *(every year)* "Olimpika Tago"-n *(an Olympic Day-acc)*

In addition to ordinary spelling errors and grammatical errors, we also mark semantic errors where the words' lemma itself, rather than its spelling, inflection or affixation is wrong. Lemma errors amount to 17.0% of all errors in the corpus and come in two types, local and contextual. The first are lemmas that look like Esperanto, but aren't – with entire lemmas or word parts inspired by other languages, e.g. *net|komunumo* (internet community) instead of *ret|*

komunumo, where the morpheme for "internet" is wrongly assumed to be 'net-', a root that in Esperanto only has the meaning of 'after costs' (as in *net profit*). Once known to the system, this kind of lemma error can be safely corrected with a dictionary look-up.

Contextual lemma errors, on the other hand. are arguably the most difficult type of real-word errors, comprising confusion errors, false friends and word choice errors based on a wrong meaning. In all of these, lemma substitution has to be performed with few or no surface clues other than valency patterns and the semantics of the surrounding words, which is why this kind of error can only be handled with complex and lemma-specific CG rules. Thus, (r5) lemma-corrects *'oferi'* (to sacrifice) into *'oferti'* (to offer) if it has an accusative (ACC) dependent (c) that is not a person (HUM-pers), animal (<A[a-z]*>), anatomical (<an.*>) or 'comfort':

```
(r5) ADD (@:BASE-oferti) TARGET ("oferi")+AKT
(c N/PROP/PRON + ACC LINK NOT 0 HUM-pers
OR(<A[a-z]*>r) OR (<an.*>r) OR ("komforto"))
```

Tag	Error	%
lemma	non-word lemma error	10.5
:BASE-xxx	real-word lemma confusion, inflecting	62.3
:xxx	real-word lemma confusion, non-inflecting	27.2
		100

Table 2: Lemma errors

Contextual lemma errors are 9x more frequent in the corpus than non-word lemma errors (table 2). About 70% of the former are inflecting lemmas and need postprocessing after substitution. The remainder are function word errors, mostly wrong use of a preposition, a common example being the confusion of *'de'* (*la aŭto de amiko* – the car of a friend) and the "quantitative" preposition *'da'* (*botelo da vino* – a bottle of wine).

Another contextual and CG-managed error type are insertions and deletions, with 5.7% and 2.6% of error markings, respectively. A typical rule is (r6), inserting the conjunction *'ke'* (that) after af finite verb form (VFIN) of *'pensi'* (think), if it has a left subject dependent (cl &SUBJ>) and is followed (*1) by another left subject (and then its verb) without interfering material other than prenominals (NON-PRE-N/ADV). The conjunction is obligatory in Esperanto and omitting it is a common "English" (or, for that matter, Scandinavian) L1 interference error:

```
(r6) ADDCOHORT
("<ke>" "ke" KS &SUB @insert)
AFTER ("pensi") + VFIN
(cl &SUBJ>)
(*1 &SUBJ> BARRIER NON-PRE-N/ADV OR CLB-
ORD LINK *1 VFIN BARRIER CLB)
```

Insertions concern mainly missing definite articles (69%), followed by prepositions (23%), while deletions are more diverse, with a 21% article share. The frequency of article errors is likely to depend on the L1 of the speaker. Slavic languages, for instance, make considerably less use of the definite article than Esperanto, and in Mandarin Chinese the closest equivalent to a definite article is a demonstrative.

Finally, we mark punctuation errors, the vast majority being comma errors (15.1% of all error markings), with sentence splitting and other punctuation accounting for under 0.5%. Comma correction has been implemented at the clause level only[18], as group level commas (e.g. lists and appositions) do not present a problem for most language users. Because they have to take into account overall sentence structure and possible word order variation, the necessary CG rules are fairly complex, not least for clause-end commas. (r7) is such a rule, targeting the left-most adjacent dependent (&>A, &>N, &ARG>, &ADVL>) of a main-clause finite verb (&FV) – or the verb itself - with a left context of a subclause finite verb (&FS) without a left argument or anouther main-clause verb coming in between. The real rule has seven NEGATE contexts as a safety measure, only two of which are shown here, a crossing prepositional argument dependency (&P<) and an un-accounted-for left subject (&SUBJ>).

```
(r7) ADD (@comma-FSend) TARGET &>A OR &>N
OR &ARG/ADVL> OR &FV
(*1S &FV BARRIER &<ARG/ADVL OR CLB OR &MV
LINK NOT 0 @inf)
(NOT -1 &>A OR &>N OR &ARG/ADVL> OR
KOMMA OR CLB-ORD OR KC OR HYFEN)
(*-1 &FS BARRIER &ARG/ADVL> OR &FV LINK NOT
0 &FV)
```

[18] There are no official comma rules for Esperanto, but classical literature mostly uses a central-European grammatical comma separating clauses with start, end and coordination commas. This is also the editorial strategy of the international Esperanto journal *Monato* (https://www.monato.be/konvencioj.php#inter).

```
(NEGATE *1 &P< BARRIER PRP)
(NEGATE *-1 &SUBJ>& BARRIER VFIN)
```

There are five types of clause separation commas, plus a marker for a wrong/spurious comma:

Tag	Error	%
FS-start	start of subclause	64.5
FS-end	end of subclause	4.5
FSco	subclause coordination	2.8
FMco	main clause coordination	24.1
contrast	contrasting comma	2.1
comma	unspecified	0.5
no-comma	wrong/spurious comma	1.5
		100

Table 3: Comma errors

The 2/3 dominance of the subclause start comma can be explained by the fact that subclauses are more likely to be appended than prepended. In addition it may be a factor that this type of comma is not used in English-speaking countries.

4 Pedagogical considerations

Apart from a machine-learning perspective, the EspEraro corpus has mainly a pedagogical purpose, not least allowing teachers to find and contrast typical error examples, and for students, to understand usage patterns. In this context, some error types are more important than others. The arguably most stigmatizing[19] error in Esperanto is not using the accusative *-n* correctly. It is therefore an advantage that case error categories are strongly represented in the corpus (60% of all grammatical errors). In addition, the fact that 9 subtypes are distinguished (5 @acc, 4 @nom) has explicative value, as mixing examples (e.g. object with adverbial uses) would make it more difficult for the learner to grasp the usage scenarios for the accusative ending.

Another pedagogically important topic in the corpus are confusion word pairs and false friends (e.g. *letero/litero* ['mail letter' vs. 'a-z letter'], *necesi/bezoni* [be necessary vs. need]). Here, contextualized error examples (i.e. whole sentences) not only help to perceive usage differences, but also to implicitly define the two different meanings through the example's semantic context. Because of its text book sources, the corpus has a comprehensive coverage of this type of error, with ~350 individual confusion pair lemmas.

In terms of usage patterns it should be born in mind that the corpus dowith es not *only* contain erroneous uses of a problematic lemma, but also *correct* uses. Thus, the partitive preposition *'da'* is represented with 8 *de-->da* corrections, 5 insertions and 14 *da-->de* corrections, but also with 211 ordinary, correct occurrences. The material could be used to extract a usage snapshot or to create insertion exercises, like the red 7x7 and 8x8 combination matrices below (e.g *suficê/multe/... de (→ da) seĝoj/mono/...* etc.):

{suficê | multe | miliono | deko | guto | tino | sako}
[enough, much, million, ten_noun, drop, vat]

de → da

{seĝoj | mono | infanoj | lingvoj | sango | ligno | ovoj}
[chairs, money, children, languages, blood, wood, eggs]

and/or, for the opposite confusion error:

{plimulto| plejmulto| specoj | malpermeso | ĉenoj | 68% | manko | loĝantaro}
[larger part, majority, types, interdiction, chains, 68%, lack, inhabitants]

da → de

{homoj | kubanoj | floroj | circumcido | bambuaroj | voĉdonoj | tempo | iom malpli ol}
[people, cubans, flowers, circumcision, bamboo bushes, votes, time, a little more than]

and, finally, for the omission error:

Ø → da

centoj (da) miloj [hundreds of millions]
pli (da) pomoj [more apples]
milionoj (da) gastoj [millions of guests]
pli (da) amikojn [more friends_accusative]

5 Outlook

With the large scope of manually revised error types contained in the current version of the corpus, and given the detailed CG analysis of error contexts, we hope EspEraro will fulfill its purpose as a teaching and development tool.

[19] The error has its own Facebook page as "most liked and hated error": https://www.facebook.com/akuzativo

However, the corpus is too selective and too small to permit true linguistic-statistical research on the real-life distribution of Esperanto errors. So future work should trade quality against quantity for this purpose, creating a large, multi-genre sister corpus of at least 10 million words, with automatic annotation only, allowing diachronic studies, genre comparison and – given the necessary meta data - an examination of the influence of an author's L1.

Acknowledgments

Lingvohelpilo-2 is a GrammarSoft ApS project and has been made possible by funding received from the Esperantic Studies Foundation (ESF). Current development has drawn on prior work carried out during the first Lingvohelpilo project[20] 2008-2010, as well as improvements made to the spellchecker and its underlying EspGram parser in the interim.

References

Reima Al-Jarf. 2010. *Spelling Error Corpora in EFL*. 7. 6-15. 10.17265/1539-8072/2010.01.002.

Þórunn Arnardóttir, Isidora Glisic, Annika Simonsen, Lilja Stefánsdóttir, and Anton Ingason. 2022. Error Corpora for Different Informant Groups: Annotating and Analyzing Texts from L2 Speakers, People with Dyslexia and Children. In *Proceedings of the 19th International Conference on Natural Language Processing (ICON)*, pp. 245–252, New Delhi, India. ACL

Eckhard Bick. 2007. Tagging and Parsing an Artificial Language: An Annotated Web-Corpus of Esperanto, In: *Proceedings of Corpus Linguistics 2007, Birmingham, UK*. Electronically published at (http://ucrel.lancs.ac.uk/publications/CL2007/, Nov. 2007)

Eckhard Bick. 2023. VISL & CG-3: Constraint Grammar on the Move: An application-driven paradigm. In: Arvi Hurskainen, Kimmo Koskenniemi & Tommi Pirinen (eds.), *Rule-Based Language Technology*. NEALT Monograph Series vol. 2, pp. 112-140. University of Tartu. ISSN 1736-6291

M. Gamon, M. Chodorow, C. Leacock, and J. Tetreault. 2013. Using learner corpora for automatic error detection and correction. In A. Diaz-Negrillo, N. Ballier, & P. Thompson (Eds.), *Automatic Treatment and Analysis of Learner Corpus Data*. Amsterdam and Philadelphia: John Benjamins, pp. 127–149.

Jared Lichtarge, Chris Alberti, Shankar Kumar, Noam Shazeer, Niki Parmar, and Simon Tong. 2019. Corpora Generation for Grammatical Error Correction. In Proceedings of NAACL 2019: Human Language Technologies, Vol. 1, pp. 3291–3301, Minneapolis, Minnesota. ACL.

Ekaterina Rakhilina, Anastasia Vyrenkova, Elmira Mustakimova, Alina Ladygina, and Ivan Smirnov. Building a learner corpus for Russian. 2016. In *Proceedings of the joint workshop on NLP for Computer Assisted Language Learning and NLP for Language Acquisition* at SLTC, Umeå, 16th November 2016. http://aclweb.org/anthology/W16-65

[20] For information about this project and access to the old tool, see https://edu.visl.dk/lingvohelpilo/

Rule-based Surface Realization of Romanian Weak Pronouns

Ciprian-Virgil Gerstenberger
UiT The Arctic University of Norway
`ciprian.gerstenberger@gmail.com`

Abstract

Due to its reliance on context and intricate grammatical rules, the Romanian weak pronoun system presents a challenge not only for language learners – both native and non-native speakers – but also for linguistic description and computational processing.

The present work addresses the challenges of Romanian weak pronouns from a computational processing perspective. Accordingly, it has three main goals: (1) to present the implementation of a rule-based model for generating contextually accurate surface forms of Romanian weak pronouns, (2) to describe the compilation of a database of relevant inputs for testing surface realization, and (3) to test the effectiveness of the model.

This serves as a proof of concept, demonstrating both the transparency and the effectiveness of the model when based on an appropriate linguistic description.

1 Introduction

Romanian weak pronouns (henceforth, RWPs), commonly referred to as clitics, exhibit a variety of surface forms governed by intricate, contextually dependent morphophonological rules. As a result, they pose challenges not only for linguistic description but also for computational modeling and natural language processing (henceforth, NLP).

Despite extensive research on Romanian clitics within various theoretical frameworks – including Generative Grammar, as explored by Dobrovie-Sorin (1999), Somesfalean (2007), and Săvescu Ciucivara (2009); Lexical Functional Grammar (LFG), as proposed by Barbu and Toivonen (2018); Head-Driven Phrase Structure Grammar (HPSG), as discussed in Monachesi (2001) and Monachesi (2005); various Optimality Theory (OT) models, advanced by Popescu (2000), Sasaki and Căluianu (2000), Legendre (2001), Popescu (2003), and Cherecheș (2014); and Dynamic Syntax, as promoted by Klein (2007) – there remains a need for practical, computational tools that can accurately generate and predict their usage in real-world contexts.

The current study addresses this gap by focusing on the creation of a rule-based model designed to handle the surface realization of RWPs, tested using a specialized input database. This, in turn, contributes to the broader goal of enhancing computational linguistic applications for Romanian.

2 Romanian Weak Pronouns

As with other Romance languages, Romanian employs a pronominal system that includes both strong pronouns and weak (or clitic) pronouns. Romanian has a complex clitic system with fully marked case, number, and gender distinctions, comprising both personal and reflexive RWPs. Moreover, there are some Romanian weak verb (henceforth, RWV) forms of the verb *to be* that behave similarly to RWPs. RWPs can appear in both syllabic and asyllabic forms. Their syllabic surface form, as well as the requirement for asyllabicity (obligatory sandhi) or the possibility of asyllabicity (optional sandhi), is determined by their contexts of occurrence. Sandhi refers to phonological adjustments that occur at morpheme or word boundaries, influenced by various factors. The asyllabic (and thus reduced) RWP

Proceedings of the 9th Workshop on Constraint Grammar and Finite State NLP, pages 9–18
March 5, 2025

forms are referred to as sandhi forms.

RWPs occur in a fixed order of up to three elements [RWP_*dat_ethicus* < RWP_*dat* < RWP_*acc*] in clitic clusters (or clitic sequences), alongside other clitics such as negation, auxiliary verbs, or adverbial particles (ex. 1). The cluster can occur both in preverbal position (e.g., in declarative sentences, ex. 2) and postverbal position (e.g., in imperative sentences, ex. 3), with the exception of negation and adverbial particles, which can occur only preverbally.

(1) Nu ni le- ai
not cl_1.pl.dat cl_3.pl.acc.f have_2.sg.pres
mai dat.
more given
«You didn't give them to us anymore.»

(2) Mi le dai
cl_1.sg.dat cl_3.pl.acc.f give_2.sg.pres
acum.
now
«You give them to me now.»

(3) Dă -mi -le acum!
give_2.sg.imp cl_1.sg.dat cl_3.pl.acc.f now
«Give them to me now!»

(4) Le dai mere.
cl_3.pl.dat give_2.sg.pres apple_pl.acc
«You give apples to them.»

Romanian exhibits various types of ambiguity that complicate the interpretation of the RWP data, such as case syncretism between accusative (*le* in ex. 2) and dative (*le* in ex. 4) plural, part-of-speech homonymy (between the dative-reflexive RWP *și* and the conjunction *și* «and» in ex. 5), phoneme-grapheme ambiguity (syllabic form [mi] in ex. 6 vs. asyllabic form with a glide [mi̯] in ex. 7), as well as hyphen ambiguity (marking asyllabicity in *mi-o* in ex. 7 vs. marking postverbality in *dă-mi-le* in ex. 3).

(5) Și le cumpără
cl_3.sg.dat.refl cl_3.pl.acc.f buy_3.sg.pres
și și le
and_conj cl_3.sg.dat.refl cl_3.pl.acc.f
revinde.
resell_3.sg.pres
«He/she buys them for him-/herself and resells them for him-/herself»

(6) Mi -l dai.
cl_1.sg.dat cl_3.sg.acc.m give_2.sg.pres
«You give it to me.»

(7) Mi -o dai.
cl_1.sg.dat cl_3.sg.acc.f give_2.sg.pres
«You give her/it to me.»

(8) Îmi dai cartea.
cl_1.sg.dat give_2.sg.pres book_def.sg.acc
«You give me the book.»

(9) Dă -mi cartea!
give_2.sg.imp cl_1.sg.dat book_def.sg.acc
«Give me the book!»

As a general observation, syllable reduction, whether obligatory or optional, always occurs in the rightmost RWP. Obligatory sandhi to the following item, to the right, is triggered by the occurrence of an auxiliary verb starting with a vowel (e.g., *am, a, aș, oi, om*) or the 3.SG.ACC.F RWP form *o* (*mi-o* in ex. 7) .

Obligatory sandhi to the preceding item, to the left, occurs if the context for obligatory sandhi to the right is not present and the underlying form (see Section 3) of the rightmost item ends in *i* or *u*. If the preceding item is also an RWP it serves as syllabic host for the rightmost RWP (*mi-l* in ex. 6). If the rightmost RWP is the only item in the sequence it surface as *î*-prothetic form in preverbal position (*îmi* in ex. 8). In postverbal position, the verb functions as the syllabic host (*dă-mi* in ex. 9).

The RWP underlying forms *ni, li, vi* for PL.DAT exhibit a special behavior: occurring as single RWPs, thus in both the rightmost and leftmost position, they surface as their accusative counterparts *ne, vă,* and *le*, respectively – an instance of the aforementioned case syncretism (*le* in ex. 4). In other cluster positions, the surface forms remain identical to the underlying forms (*ni* in ex. 1).

When obligatory sandhi is not possible but specific contextual conditions are met, Romanian RWPs can undergo optional sandhi. This means that they may reduce (asyllabic *le* in ex. 11), but such a reduction is not compulsory (syllabic *le* in ex. 10). Optional sandhi to the following item, to the right, is possible if the following item starts with an unstressed vowel (ex. 11). Similarly, some RWPs in a sequence of length one can optionally attach to the preceding item, to the left, if the preceding item ends with an unstressed vowel (*să-mi* in ex. 12). In the same context, the RWP can also surface as an î-prothetic form (*îmi* in 13).

(10) Le aduci mere
cl_3.pl.dat bring_2.sg.pres apple_pl.acc
«You bring them apples.»

(11) Le- aduci mere
cl_3.pl.dat bring_2.sg.pres apple_pl.acc

«You bring them apples.»

(12) Vreau sǎ -mi
want_1.sg.pres that cl_1.sg.dat
dai mere.
give_2.sg.pres apples
«I want you to give me apples.»

(13) Vreau sǎ îmi
want_1.sg.pres that cl_1.sg.dat
dai mere.
give_2.sg.pres apples
«I want you to give me apples.»

3 Model description

The computational implementation of a theoretical model serves as a bridge between abstract concepts and practical applications, providing a platform to explore, validate, and extend the capabilities of the model. In linguistics, where numerous frameworks come with diverse theoretical constructs, translating these abstract models into computational terms becomes essential (see, for instance, Bender and Langendoen, 2010).

Although numerous computational tools for linguistics are available – such as Hayes et al. (2013) for OT, Kaplan et al. (2004) for LFG, Copestake (2001) for HPSG, to name a few –, none of the theoretical approaches to RWPs mentioned in Section 1 have attempted to demonstrate how these frameworks can be computationally implemented and systematically validated.

In Gerstenberger (2022), I provided comprehensive description of RWPs and their contexts of occurrence using transparently intersubjectively testable linguistics features based on their (a)syllabicity. Granted, the syllable is notoriously difficult to define in a universally agreed-upon way – is it primarily a unit of speech production (articulation), perception, or both? (cf., for instance, Ohala, 2008), but it is widely recognized as a fundamental building block in phonological theory.

Unlike Dobrovie-Sorin and Giurgea's (2013:p. 266) claim that „clitic forms are underlyingly asyllabic or syllabic", Popescu's (2003:p. 154) claim of an unspecified underlying mora, or Klein's (2007:p. 77) use of clusters with *î*-prothetic forms as model input, I propose a model in which all underlying representations are uniformly syllabic (see Table 1).

The model I propose for handling RWPs is similar to the generative approach in Chomsky and Halle (1968) and the two-level morphology in Koskenniemi (1983), as it employs two different levels of representation as well as a set of rules for mapping between the underlying and surface levels.

While the underlying representations are theoretical linguistic entities, the input forms are their computational linguistic counterparts – concrete strings that can be processed.

Given the case syncretism between accusative and dative plural RWP forms presented in Section 2 – *ni* ⇒ *ne* (syllabic) and then *ne* (syllabic) ⇒ *ne-* (asyllabic), as well as that the observation that the obligatory sandhi to the right has higher precedence than the obligatory sandhi to the left, a consecutive rule set, as presented for XFST in Beesley and Karttunen (2003), seems better suited to implement these rules.

The key idea when modeling RWP phenomena is to account for the position of a clitic in the clitic sequence: is the clitic in the rightmost position or not? Next, it is necessary to identify the correct contextual features for distinguishing between obligatory and optional sandhi. The asyllabic RWP forms are marked by vowel loss, hyphen addition, or both, while the postverbal position is characterized by the addition of hyphens between all items in the clitic sequence that follow the verb.

The following XFST grammar fragment provides definitions and rules for modeling the obligatory sandhi to the right for all RWPs that are followed by an auxiliary verb starting with a vowel or by the RWP form *o*.

```
define V_RWP "o";
define ReduceHighV_RWP "mi" | "ți" | "i" |
    "și";
define DeleteHighV_RWP "lu";
define SubstitueHighV_RWP "ni" | "vi" | "li";
define HighV_RWP ReduceHighV_RWP |
    DeleteHighV_RWP | SubstitueHighV_RWP;
define DeleteLowV_RWP "mă" | "se" | "vă";
define LowV_RWP DeleteLowV_RWP | "te" | "ne" |
     "le";
define Syllabic_RWP HighV_RWP | LowV_RWP;
define V_Initial_Aux "am" | "ai" | "a" | ...";
define C_Initial_Aux "voi" | "vei" | "va" | "
    vom" | ...;
define Aux V_Initial_Aux | C_Initial_Aux;
define Is_Obligatory_Host V_Initial_Aux |
    V_RWP;
define RWP V_RWP | Syllabic_RWP;
define Rightmost_RWP Syllabic_RWP .#. -
```

Number	Accusative					Dative					Verb *a fi*	
	1p	2p	3p.m	3p.f	3p.refl	1p	2p	3p.m	3p.f	3p.refl	1p.pres	3p.pres
Sg	/mə/	/te/	/lu/	/o/	/se/	/mi/	/tsi/	/i/	/i/	/ʃi/	/su/	/i/
Pl	/ne/	/və/	/i/	/le/	/se/	/ni/	/vi/	/li/	/li/	/ʃi/	–	/su/

Tabela 1: Underlying forms as input for the surface form generation of RWPs and RWV *a fi* «to be»

```
    Syllabic_RWP .#. Syllabic_RWP;
define Remove_Vowel
    (DeleteLowV_RWP | DeleteHighV_RWP) -> (""
    / [aeiouă] _ )
    / .#. Is_Obligatory_Host;
define Substitute_Form
    "ni" -> "ne" / _ Rightmost_RWP .#. ||
    "vi" -> "vă" / _ Rightmost_RWP .#. ||
    "li" -> "le" / _ Rightmost_RWP .#.;
define Add_Right_Hyphen Rightmost_RWP -> "-" /
     _ Is_Obligatory_Host;
define Asyllabic_Transformation Remove_Vowel
    || Substitute_Form || Add_Right_Hyphen;
regex Asyllabic_Transformation;
```

First, groups of items with the same behavior are defined. `ReduceHighV_RWP` items have the same orthographic string in both their syllabic and asyllabic forms. `DeleteHighV_RWP` and `DeleteLowV_RWP` items lose the vowel as asyllabic forms, as expressed in the rule `Remove_Vowel`. `SubstitueHighV_RWP` items change they form accordingly in the rule `Substitute_Form`, reflecting the aforementioned case syncretism.

The positional information – whether an RWP is the rightmost in the sequence – is modeled by the rule *Rightmost_RWP*: a rightmost RWP is not followed by any other RWP, which is expressed using set subtraction.

In the context of the obligatory host to the right, the rule `Add_Right_Hyphen` ensures that the correct orthographic forms are produced as surface forms.

4 Model implementation

While the XFST grammar fragment in the previous section is a proof that some linguistic phenomena described in Section 2 can be translated into XFST rules, the concrete implementation has been done in Python. There are some non-negligeable reasons for Python:

- Python allows for more expressive rule implementations.
- Python has excellent debugging and testing tools.
- Python has a rich ecosystem for NLP such as spaCy, NLTK, Stanza.
- Python syntax is cleaner and easier to read than XFST syntax.
- Python scripts can be easily documented, shared, deployed, or packaged.

The task of the surface form generation module is to produce the correct spelling of each RWP within its specific context. Since the proposed model takes syllabic RWPs as input, the following operations are performed: deleting a vowel, changing a vowel, adding a sandhi-marking hyphen, adding a prothetic *î*, and adding postverbal hyphens.

The module expects the input to provide all necessary linguistic information for each form in a given context. During the generation process, the procedure first checks the features of each item and applies the constraints on obligatory sandhi to the right, then to the left, followed by those on optional sandhi. For additional surface form adjustments, certain gerund and imperative forms may adapt to the context. If no sandhi constraints apply, the syllabic underlying RWP forms remain unchanged.

Since the main task of this project was a proof of concept – namely, to demonstrate that the linguistic description of RWPs in Gerstenberger (2022) can be implemented transparently – *spaCy*[1], an open-source software library for advanced NLP in Python was chosen for this task. Not only do *spaCy* Doc objects contain default linguistic annotations, such as part-of-speech tags and positional information of specific tokens in context, but the linguistic structure can also be adapted, extended,

[1]`https://spacy.io/`

and customized for specific types of annotation. When run on the input, all annotations can be queried and checked for contextual values, allowing operations to be performed on each token.

The input sentence (see, e.g., Figure 2) is analyzed using a «fine-tuned» *spaCy* pipeline created specifically for this test input set. As shown in the code fragment in Figure 1, the Python rules operate on each token in the spaCy Doc object.

For instance, the code checks whether the current token is a *Linear Order Part*, as defined in Gerstenberger (2007), meaning that it can occur in both preverbal and postverbal positions. If this condition is met, it further checks whether the token is an RWP or an RWV to determine whether additional operations should be performed on the input string. Along with default value checks on the current token – such as its current position and contextual elements – custom functions like `token._.is_rwp`, `token._.is_rwv`, and `is_rightmost_in_cluster(token)` have been implemented for this task. To address the dative/accusative case syncretism in the plural, an `interim_form` mapping has been employed. The entire rule set is freely available from `https://github.com/ciprian-NO/rb_rwp_generation/blob/main/generate_rwp_surface_forms.ipynb`.

To test the effectiveness of the module, I created a test input database covering all relevant RWP phenomena described in Section 2.

5 Test database creation

Evidently, the design of the test input database is driven by the RWP surface realization model proposed. The structure of a database entry is a tuple of <INPUT, {TARGET$_1$,..., TARGET$_n$}>, where the input string contains the syllabic input, i.e., the underlying representation of RWPs and the set contains all possible output variants. For example, for the curse-like expression *Înțepeni-i-s-ar toate oasele!* («May all his/her bones stiffen!»), the input is `[Înțepeni i se ar toate oasele!]`, created by removing all hyphens that indicate postverbality or asyllabicity. Furthermore, the obligatory asyllabic surface form *s* has been replaced by the syllabic underlying form *se*. Due to grapheme-phoneme ambiguities in RWPs 2, the RWP form *i* remains unchanged because it can stay both for a syllabic and an asyllabic form.

As mentioned above (see Section 2), optional sandhi refers to phonological adjustments at morpheme or word boundaries that may be influenced by factors such as individual speech patterns (idiolect), social or regional dialects (sociolect, regiolect), or the formality level of speech (speech register). As for different output targets, these are basically the result of optional sandhi, that can occur in different contexts.

Figure 2 shows a database entry with only one target. In such an entry, the `source` string is identical to the `target` string, *Arată-ne muzeul!* («Show us the museum!»): both contain the correct surface form of the RWPs.

In database entries that contain multiple targets reflecting optional sandi, e.g., for the sentences *De ce îi dai mere?* («Why are you giving him/her apples?») in Figure 3 or *O împușcă în inimă.* («He/She shoots her in the heart.») in Figure 4, the *source* string is only one of the different targets.

RWP configurations are complex due to their syntactic positioning, morphological behavior, and interactions with other elements in the sentence. When building a specialized test input database for testing the surface realization of RWPs, several key linguistic and structural factors (see Section 2) must be considered, such as: person, number, gender, and case of RWPs, cluster length, etc.

The test input database has been primarily created based on examples from Gerstenberger (2022) and the relevant literature cited therein. RWP examples that were not complete sentences have been minimally expanded into full sentences (the *source* string in a database entry), typically by adding an adverb (e.g., *cumpără-l* «buy it» becomes *Cumpără-l repede!* «Buy it quickly!»). Some RWP sequences are repeated in different contexts to test surface realization in cases of optional sandhi.

The database contains 352 input strings and 470 target sentences, distributed as follows: 257 sets with one target output, 80 sets with two target variants, 7 sets with three variants,

```python
# 1. current token is a Linear Order Part (LOP), i.e., can occur both pre- and post-verbally
if token._.is_linear_order_part:
    is_postverbal_token = not is_preverbal(token) and not r_nbor.pos_ == 'VERB'
    if is_postverbal_token:
        postverbal_hyphen = HYPHEN_TOKEN.text

    # 1.1 current token is a Romanian Weak Pronoun (RWP) or a Romanian Weak Verb (RWV)
    if  token._.is_rwp or token._.is_rwv:
        # 1.1.1 RWP rightmost item in the cluster
        if is_rightmost_in_cluster(token):

            # cope with ni => ne, vi => vă, and li => le
            interim_form = get_interim_form(token.lower_)

            # 1.1.1.1 obligatory sandhi to the right
            if r_nbor._.is_obligatory_host:
                surface_form = get_asyllabic_form(interim_form, "OBLIGATORY") + HYPHEN_TOKEN.text
                surface_forms.append(postverbal_hyphen+surface_form)

            # 1.1.1.2 no obligatory host to the right
            else:

                # 1.1.1.2.1 obligatory sandhi to the left for the u- and i-forms (lu ==> -l, mi ==> -mi)
                if l_nbor._.is_rwp:
                    # 1.1.1.2.1.1 e- or ă-forms
                    if ('e' in interim_form) or ('ă' in interim_form):
                        surface_form = interim_form
                        surface_forms.append(postverbal_hyphen+surface_form)
                        ## check for optional sandhi
                        if r_nbor._.vowel_initial_char and r_nbor._.vowel_initial and not \
                           r_nbor._.is_first_syllable_stressed and not r_nbor.lower_.startswith('o') and not\
                           r_nbor.lower_.startswith('e'):
                            surface_form = get_asyllabic_form(interim_form, "OPTIONAL") + HYPHEN_TOKEN.text
                            surface_forms.append(postverbal_hyphen+surface_form)
```

Figura 1: Example of RWP surface generation rules implemented in Python

and 8 sets with four. The main features of the RWPs are summarized in Table 2. Even if a database with only 352 input string might seem small, it contains all relevant phenomena for handling with RWPs.

Both the input string and target sets were manually created. The input string is generated by replacing all instances of RWP surface forms with their underlying forms and removing any hyphens or prothetic *î* in the example sentence, representing an abstraction process. In contrast, creating the target set involves generating all possible variants of the input string, representing an instantiation process.

For contexts involving RWPs, all possible combinations have been created. However, in cases of optional sandhi without RWPs, only those variants covered by the rules implemented for RWP contexts have been generated. Moreover, since there is no consensus on what precisely triggers the spell-out of different variants in optional sandhi, the decision was made to include all potential variants, even though some may be more acceptable than others depending on the context.

When selecting examples for the test database, I avoided using RWP sequences that are not widely accepted, such as coordinated RWPs (see Dobrovie-Sorin and Giurgea, 2013, p. 262) or examples of RWP clitic sequences involving marginally acceptable Person Case Constraint (PCC), a constraint that restricts the co-occurrence of certain clitic pronouns, specifically based on two features: person and case (cf. Bonet, 1994).

While not aiming to exhaust all possible RWP combinations, I sought to cover all relevant phenomena described in Gerstenberger (2022). Moreover, since this database was created manually and has been incrementally corrected, it is not immune to errors, either in linguistic judgment or spelling.

As a final remark, the same input test database is intended for use in testing statistically-based generative methods, more specific, Generative Pre-Trained Transformers (GPTs). Given their widespread popularity and apparent versatility, I decided to test the GPT large language models provided by OpenAI (2024). The goal of using a shared test in-

Feature	Preverbal forms	Postverbal forms	Example
RWP sequence length	L1: 280 L2: 79 L3: 16	L1: 71 L2: 31 L3: 7	`Postverbal L2` *Dă-mi-le acum!* «Give them to me now!»
	Obligatory î-prothetic forms	**Optional î-prothetic forms**	
Î-prothetic contexts (Only preverbal L1)	25	`î-prothetic forms: 43` `no î-prothetic forms: 50`	`Optional î-prothetic form` *De ce îmi dai mere?* «Why are you giving me apples?»
	Obligatory forms	**Optional sandhi contexts**	
No *î*-prothetic contexts	267	`RWP as syllabic host: 32` `Context item as syllabic host: 50`	`Obligatory RWP forms` *De ce mi le dai?* «Why are you giving them to me?»
	Syllabic context items	**Asyllabic context items**	
Optional sandhi contexts with RWP as possible syllabic host	15	17	`RWP as syllabic host` *N-o văd bine.* «I don't see her/it well.»
	Syllabic RWP forms	**Asyllabic RWP forms**	
Optional sandhi contexts with context item as possible syllabic host	25	25	`Context item as syllabic host` *El ne-arată muzeul.* «He shows us the museum.»

Tabela 2: Distribution of RWP features of target sentences in the test database

put database is to establish a foundation for fair comparison and evaluation between rule-based and GPT-based approaches.

6 Feature annotation and validation

The model relies on fine-grained linguistic information about both the currently processed item and its context, which necessitates that the input data be linguistically annotated accordingly.

As already mentioned, for processing the entire set of 352 input sentences, I chose to use *spaCy* for several reasons:

- it offers multi-language support for over 75 languages, including Romanian[2];
- it offers a hybrid approach, i.e., it supports both machine learning models and linguistic rules;
- it is highly customizable and extensible (e.g., via Custom Token Attributes such as `is_obligatory_host`.)

To address both obligatory and optional sandhi in RWP surface realization, the *spaCy* annotations have been extended with a set of functions that enrich token annotation with features for grapheme-phoneme disambiguation (`vowel_final_char` vs. `vowel_final`) and indicate whether an initial vowel is stressed (`is_first_syllable_stressed`).

Another set of functions has been devised to add high-level annotations, such as `is_rwp`, `is_rightmost_in_cluster`, or `is_obligatory_host`. These functions rely on default morphosyntactic annotations and are designed to simplify the validation of contextual features for generating the appropriate RWP form.

Finally, to ensure that hyphens indicating asyllabicity, postverbality, or both are assigned according to official writing conventions, the annotations `is_linear_order_part` and `is_preverbal` have been added to the default *spaCy* token features. In contrast to preverbal position (ex. 2), all items in a cluster – including RWPs and auxiliary verbs – are connected to the main verb by hyphens in postverbal position (ex. 3).

Each input string is annotated using the *spaCy* module, extended with functions for additional features, and the results are serialized in JSON format. Task-relevant annotations are then manually corrected, and finally, the JSON structures are converted to *spaCy*'s binary format. Since only task-relevant annotations are manually corrected, other annotations may contain errors.

7 Output testing

As with the development of any other handcrafted grammar, the implementation of the RWP surface generation module was an iterative process involving careful analysis, rule refinement, and extensive testing to ensure that linguistic patterns were accurately captured. Each iteration required revisiting existing rules, adding new ones, and addressing edge cases.

The spaCy-annotated, manually corrected

[2]`https://spacy.io/models/ro`

```
"ex021": {
  "ex021_input": "Arată ni muzeul!",
  "ex021_source": "Arată-ne muzeul!",
  "targets": {
    "ex021_t01": "Arată-ne muzeul!"
  }
}
```

Figura 2: Database entry with one target

```
"ex049": {
  "ex049_input": "De ce i dai mere?",
  "ex049_source": "De ce îi dai mere?",
  "targets": {
    "ex049_t01": "De ce îi dai mere?",
    "ex049_t02": "De ce-i dai mere?"
  }
}
```

Figura 3: Database entry with two targets

```
"ex242": {
  "ex242_input": "O împușcă în inimă.",
  "ex242_source": "O împușcă în inimă.",
  "targets": {
    "ex242_t01": "O împușcă în inimă.",
    "ex242_t02": "O-mpușcă în inimă.",
    "ex242_t03": "O împușcă-n inimă.",
    "ex242_t04": "O-mpușcă-n inimă."
  }
}
```

Figura 4: Database entry with four targets

mini-corpus based on the input data is loaded and used to re-analyze the input so that the linguistic features needed for RWP surface generation are available for the application of the rules. Finally, the output is checked against the corresponding set of targets (see Figures 2 – 4).

Since this implementation is primarily a proof of concept – for immediate context checking –, I kept the processing as simple as possible. This simplicity means that the module has a stateless design, i.e., no «memory»: it does not retain information about the previously generated form of the current token, nor of the previously generated neighboring token. In standard Romanian orthography, hyphens can denote sandhi, postverbal clitics, or both. Given the lack of memory in the module, a hyphen may occasionally be generated twice.

For each token, a set of surface forms is generated based on its context. The set of output strings then comprises all possible combinations of these token surface forms. Cases of overgeneration are filtered out in the final step of processing, as illustrated by strings 3. and 4. below.

```
<060> . . . . . . . . . . . . . . . . .
[4 tokens] Du te încolo !
[['Du'], ['-te', '-te-'],
 ['încolo', '-ncolo'], ['!']]
  1. ('Du', '-te', 'încolo', '!')
  2. ('Du', '-te', '-ncolo', '!')
  3. ('Du', '-te-', 'încolo', '!')
  4. ('Du', '-te-', '-ncolo', '!')
. . . . . . . . . . . . . . . . . . . . .
```

The remaining correct output strings 1. *Du-te încolo!* and 2. *Du-te-ncolo!* («Go away!») are checked against the targets of the corresponding database entry in Figure 5.

```
"ex060": {
  "ex060_input": "Du te încolo!",
  "ex060_source": "Du-te încolo!",
  "targets": {
    "ex060_t01": "Du-te încolo!",
    "ex060_t02": "Du-te-ncolo!"
  }
```

Figura 5: Entry with optional sandhi targets

The hand-crafted grammar is tailored specifically for a defined input set with a particular output set, making it neither bias-free in its linguistic choice of examples or evaluations nor entirely error-free in terms of spelling or implementation. Nevertheless, it represents an attempt to faithfully implement the RWP description outlined in Gerstenberger (2022) within a computational-linguistic framework.

8 Conclusions

In this article, I presented the implementation of a model for RWP surface realization, following the linguistic description provided in Gerstenberger (2022). While Gerstenberger (2018) addresses only the realization of obligatory sandhi and does not offer a computational implementation of the algorithm, this study extends the approach by incorporating both obligatory and optional sandhi within a computational framework.

A further key contribution of this work is the compilation of a systematic set of test inputs for evaluating the model, including the linguistic annotations required to meet the implemented constraints. This computational implementation serves not only as a proof of concept but also as a robust method for validating the model, demonstrating its practical applicability, and ensuring that its predictions align with empirical data. Due to its transparency and proximity to linguistic surface forms, the model is adaptable to any constraint-based linguistic framework.

Since the resources used in this study – specifically, the input test database and the surface generation module – were created manually, they may contain errors. However, these resources are freely available at `https://github.com/ciprian-NO/rb_rwp_generation` for the research community to test, improve, and expand.

References

Roxana-Maria Barbu and Ida Toivonen. 2018. Romanian Object Clitics: Grammaticalization, agreement and lexical splits. In *Proceedings of the LFG18 Conference*, page 67–87. Stanford: CSLI Publications.

Kenneth R. Beesley and Lauri Karttunen. 2003. *Finite-State Morphology.* CSLI Publications, Stanford, CA.

Emily M. Bender and D. Terence Langendoen. 2010. Computational linguistics in support of linguistic theory. *Linguistic Issues in Language Technology*, 3.

Eulàlia Bonet. 1994. The person-case constraint: A morphological approach. *MIT Working Papers in Linguistics*, 0(22):33–52.

Anca Chereches. 2014. A Prosodic Analysis of Romanian Pronominal Clitics. In *University of Pennsylvania Working Papers in Linguistics*, volume 20. Available at https://repository.upenn.edu/pwpl/vol20/iss1/7/.

Noam Chomsky and Morris Halle. 1968. *The Sound Pattern of English.* Harper & Row.

Ann A. Copestake. 2001. Implementing typed feature structure grammars. In *CSLI lecture notes series.*

Carmen Dobrovie-Sorin. 1999. Clitics across categories: The case of Romanian. In Henk C. van Riemsdijk, editor, *Clitics in the Languages of Europe.* Mouton de Gruyter.

Carmen Dobrovie-Sorin and Ion Giurgea, editors. 2013. *A Reference Grammar of Romanian*, volume 1: The noun phrase. John Benjamins.

B. Gerlach and J. Grijzenhout, editors. 2001. *Clitics in Phonology, Morphology and Syntax.* John Benjamins.

Ciprian-Virgil Gerstenberger. 2007. A mereology-based general linearization model for surface realization. In *Proceedings of EUROLAN 2007*, University of Iaşi, Romania. Available at https://www.researchgate.net/publication/233951937_A_mereology-based_general_linearization_model_for_surface_realization.

Ciprian-Virgil Gerstenberger. 2018. A grammar for romanian weak pronoun generation. In *Languages at the Crossroads: Training, Accreditation and Context of Use. Proceedings of the 35th Edition of the International Conference of the Spanish Association of Applied Linguistics*, pages 215–226. University of Jaén. Available at https://www.researchgate.net/publication/332671041_A_Grammar_for_Romanian_weak_pronoun_generation.

Ciprian-Virgil Gerstenberger. 2022. How weak are romanian clitic pronouns? *Nordlyd*, 47(1):37–57.

Bruce Hayes, Bruce Tesar, and Kie Zuraw. 2013. OTSoft 2.5 [software package]. http://www.linguistics.ucla.edu/people/hayes/otsoft/.

Ronald M. Kaplan, John T. Maxwell III, Tracy Holloway King, and Richard Crouch. 2004. Integrating finite-state technology with deep LFG grammars. In *Proceedings of the ESSLLI'04 Workshop on Combining Shallow and Deep Processing for NLP.*

Udo-Michael Klein. 2007. *Encoding of argument structure in Romanian and SiSwati.* Ph.D. thesis, University of London. Available at http://hdl.handle.net/11858/00-001M-0000-0012-8EEC-D.

Kimmo Koskenniemi. 1983. Two-level model for morphological analysis. In *IJCAI*, volume 83, pages 683–685.

Géraldine Legendre. 2001. Positioning Romanian verbal clitics at PF. In (Gerlach and Grijzenhout, 2001).

Paola Monachesi. 2001. Clitic placement in the Romanian verbal complex. In (Gerlach and Grijzenhout, 2001).

Paola Monachesi. 2005. *The Verbal Complex in Romance: A Case Study in Grammatical Interfaces.* Oxford University Press.

John J Ohala. 2008. The emergent syllable. In *The syllable in speech production.* Taylor & Francis.

OpenAI. 2024. ChatGPT [Large Language Model]. https://chat.openai.com/chat.

Alexandra Popescu. 2000. The morphophonology of the Romanian clitic sequence. In *Lingua*, volume 110, pages 773–799. Elsevier.

Alexandra Popescu. 2003. *Morphophonologische Phänomene des Rumänischen*. Ph.D. thesis, University of Düsseldorf. Available at https://docserv.uni-duesseldorf.de/servlets/DocumentServlet?id=3187.

Kan Sasaki and Daniela Căluianu. 2000. An Optimality Theoretic Account for the Distribution of Pronominal Clitics in Romanian. Technical report, University of Tsukuba. Available at https://www.academia.edu/33668351/An_optimality_theoretic_account_for_the_distribution_of_pronominal_clitics_in_Romanian.

Stanca Somesfalean. 2007. *On the Form and Interpretation of Clitics*. Ph.D. thesis, Université du Québec à Montréal. Available at https://archipel.uqam.ca/9628/.

Oana Săvescu Ciucivara. 2009. *A Syntactic Analysis of Pronominal Clitic Clusters in Romance - The view from Romanian*. Ph.D. thesis, New York University. Available at https://www.proquest.com/docview/304954033.

Drawing Blue Lines – What can Constraint Grammar do for GEC?

Linda Wiechetek
Divvun/ UiT Norgga árktalaš universitehta
firstname.lastname@uit.no

Kevin Brubeck Unhammer
Trigram AS
firstname@trigram.no

Abstract

This paper presents the application of rule-based methods for Grammatical Error Correction (GEC) across multiple low-resource languages. We describe new functionality using the Constraint Grammar (CG) formalism, designed for detecting and correcting different types of complex grammatical errors in a range of morphologically complex languages. These errors require transformations such as reordering, word additions/deletions, and alternative choices for multiword suggestions. New perspectives are gained from end-to-end-testing – this work aims to clarify the relationship between the command-line interface used by developers and the user interfaces of our grammar checker plug-in for common word processors. We present challenges and solutions in correcting complex errors, with examples from languages like Lule Sámi, Irish, and Greenlandic, enabling linguists to adapt these methods in order to provide accurate and context-aware proofing tools for their own languages in mainstream word processors like Microsoft Word, Google Docs or LibreOffice.

1 Introduction

This work builds on Fred Karlsson's introduction to CG / Constraint Grammar (Karlsson, 1990b) (CG2), Eckhard Bick's higher doctoral dissertation (Bick, 2000) and Tino Didriksen's user manual for VISL CG3 (Didriksen, 2010). Those descriptions focus mainly on the use of the command line. However, things can look very different in popular word processing programs, where sentences are not displayed from top to bottom with each word's analysis. As programmers, the command line is our daily workplace and when things work we can easily forget that this is not the place where most writers see their texts displayed. The purpose of this article is to implement and describe how complex errors can be marked and displayed in text processing programs in a way that will be intuitive, useful and pedagogical to the writer. We will focus on proofing tool applications which are commonly used by writers, in particular grammar checkers that are substantially more complex than spellcheckers, not only from a linguistic, but also a technical point of view. The blue lines in MS Word typically stretch over more than one word, sometimes the whole sentence. Correction suggestions can include not only different spellings, but entirely different constructions. We also need ways to display correction feedback and possibilities to refer to all parts of the error in the text shown to the user.

Figure 1 illustrates how the *Divvun*[1] grammar checker works in MS Word. The text itself receives red lines for default English spellchecking, which any user of non-English text needs to turn off. The relevant grammar checking takes place in the right-hand side-bar since Microsoft does not let third-party software show feedback inside the document, even though they do not provide any alternative for e.g. Sámi speakers. Therefore the blue lines marking simple or – in this case – complex grammatical errors are found to the right of the document.

This article shows different types of complex errors in a number of languages, along with technical solutions within the CG-formalism, most of which came into being as a result of working with grammar checking. We aim to give a thorough description so that the full potential of it can be used by whoever would like to model a correction

[1] https://divvun.no/

Proceedings of the 9th Workshop on Constraint Grammar and Finite State NLP, pages 19–27
March 5, 2025 ©2025 University of Tartu Library

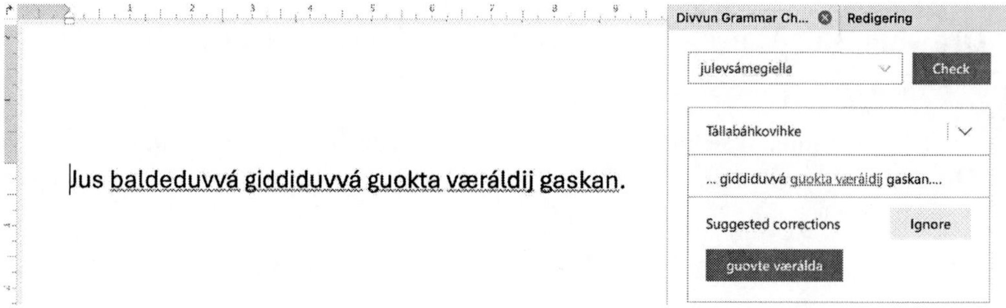

Figure 1: Divvun Grammar checking in MS Word

```
"<guokta>"
        "guokta" Num Sg Nom <W:0.0> &msyn-numphrase-sggen ID:4
        "guokta" Num <W:0.0> Sg Gen SUGGEST SUGGEST ID:4
guokta+Num+Sg+Gen       guovte
        "guokta" Num v2 Sg Acc <W:0.0> &msyn-numphrase-sggen ID:4
:
"<væráldij>"            guokta væráldij → guovte værálda
        "værált" Area/NO N <smj> <smj> Sem/Plc Pl Gen <W:0.0> &msyn-numphrase-sggen ID:5 R:$2:4 R:LEFT:4
msyn-numphrase-sggen
        "værált" Area/NO N <smj> <smj> Sem/Plc <W:0.0> Sg Gen SUGGEST SUGGEST ID:5 R:$2:4 R:LEFT:4
værált+Area/NO+N+Sg+Gen værálda,værálda,værálda
:
"<gaskan>"
        "gaskan" Po <smj> <smj> <W:0.0>
"<.>"
        "." CLB <W:0.0>
```

Figure 2: Divvun Grammar checking from the developer's perspective on the command line

grammar of their language.[2]

2 Motivation

In our work with grammatical errors, we found that our formalism lacked certain functionalities required for error detection and correction. One of them was handling multiple possible corrections of a complex error, where we have to be careful that corrections are consistent, e.g. **as the tree grow* could be corrected to *as the **trees** grow* or *as the tree **grows*** but not **as the **trees grows***. We also need to be able to reorder, add or delete words.

A large portion of grammatical errors we have encountered are *complex*, in that they require marking up several words, and corrections may have to change several words at once. For example, in North Sámi, the biggest class of grammatical errors are compound errors, where two or more adjacent words should be written as one word. The second biggest class is subject-verb agreement errors, another complex error. In Lule Sámi, we have focused on NP-internal number and case agreement, where the most complex rules target numeral phrases. These behave differently from the majority language paradigm and are hence the cause of many errors for bilingual speakers/writers. This class is relevant for all Sámi languages. Gender agreement errors in noun phrases are common errors in Irish (and in a number of other Indo-European languages as well). Greenlandic has been the showcase for word order errors, but these also appear in for example Lule Sámi, a typical SOV language that is under influence from the SVO languages Swedish and Norwegian. Greenlandic (standard SOV), faces similar pressure since speakers are typically bilingual with Danish (standard SVO). The noun phrase internal word order differs as well; Greenlandic uses N A where Danish uses A N.

3 Background

3.1 Previous work

Unlike the common assumption that all language tasks are solved by machine learning applications, much grammar checking has had and still has a rule-based foundation, even in applications that do not say this outright.[3] Bick (2015) has made

[2] A technical reference for the system is available at `https://github.com/divvun/libdivvun`

[3] The authors have personally experienced that their own work on rule-based systems has been presented as "machine

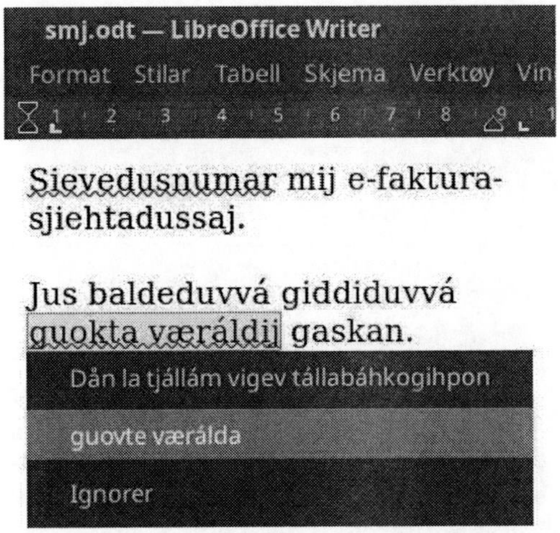

Figure 3: Divvun Grammar checking in LibreOffice (which gives writers autonomy over the choice of spelling/grammar checking providers)

several CG-based grammar checkers for Danish. *Grammatifix* (Arppe, 2000), based on CG, has been part of the Swedish MS Word since 2000. *Grammarly* is a grammar checker for English; little is published about their methods, but as Dyomkin (2015) reveals it was at that time using rules on dependency parse-trees.

3.2 Technical background

Below we describe a Constraint Grammar (CG) module for handling linguistic grammar errors. Constraint Grammar is a rule-based formalism originally developed by Karlsson (1990a); Karlsson et al. (1995). In our work, we use the free and open source implementation VISL CG-3 (Bick and Didriksen, 2015). This module is one component of a larger pipeline displayed in Figure 4. In this pipeline, the text is first tokenized and morphologically analysed with *finite-state automata* (Beesley and Karttunen, 2003) using the free and open-source toolkit HFST (Lindén et al., 2013), in particular `hfst-tokenise`, with morphologies from the Divvun/Giellatekno infrastructure (Wiechetek et al., 2022).

As described in Wiechetek et al. (2019), this step also parses consecutive words as possible compound errors (words written with extraneous spaces). A `divvun-blanktag` step adds useful tags like "start of sentence". The following Constraint Grammar tags words with valency classes, the next one disambiguates ambiguous multi-words. Then a purely mechanical step `cg-mwesplit` turns the disambiguated multi-word analyses into separate CG cohorts.[4] A second `divvun-blanktag` step tags some white-space errors. Then we run the spellchecker – this may add readings to previously unknown words. The new readings are also given valency tags by CG. Next we run a CG disambiguator and syntax tagger – this should ideally leave us with one reading per word. A second CG is used to filter out some unlikely spelling suggestions. Then we arrive at the focus of this article, the grammar checker CG (marked green in the Figure). This module contains the rules which tag grammatical errors, create suggestions and expand underlines.

The final module of the pipeline, `divvun-suggest`, uses the information given by the previous steps to look up word forms of suggestions, create readable error messages from error tags, and format it in a way that is readable to word processor plug-ins and other user interfaces.

The developer of grammar checker rules typically sees CG-formatted output when working with rules, which includes a lot of information that plug-ins do not need to see. The plug-ins need a programmatic interface which unambiguously tells them which words need underlines, and with what suggestions. This interface needs to use a format with good library support across programming languages. So `divvun-suggest` can output in two different formats: human-readable CG for the developer, and the popular data interchange format `JSON` for the plug-ins. The `JSON` format is used to communicate suggestions to plug-ins for LibreOffice, MS Word, Google Docs, web sites and newspaper publishing systems.

4 Building blocks of grammar checker rules

Before we get into the complex error examples, we give an introduction to the way grammar checker rules are written in our system. Here we describe the necessary components required to *tag* something as an error, to *suggest* a correction, to *underline* the related words of a context and to *refer* to the different parts of an error in an explanation.

We will here write a simplified rule for the common Norwegian Nynorsk agreement error in ex-

learning" or "AI" for press releases.

[4] A cohort in CG is a wordform with all its possible readings.

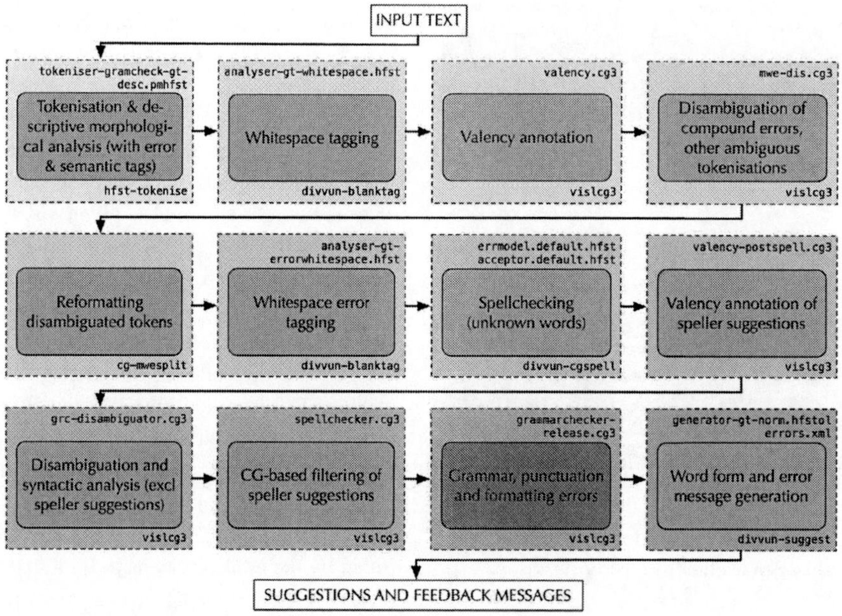

Figure 4: Modular structure of the grammar checkers

ample (1), where the wrong determiner gender is used, with correction in example (2):

(1) *å føre **eit** rekneskap
to keep an.NT account.M

(2) å føre ein rekneskap
to keep an.M account.M
'to keep accounts'

To tag this as an error, we could target the neuter determiner and give it a tag like `&det-n-nt/m-agr` if it precedes a masculine noun with the following rule, simplified for this example:

```
ADD (&det-n-nt/m-agr)
 TARGET (det nt)
 IF (1 (n m)) (NEGATE 1 (n nt)) ;
```

Tags beginning with `&` are interpreted as error tags by the `divvun-suggest` module. This rule alone will ensure the determiner is underlined in the user's word processor, but does not yet lead to a suggestion. To suggest the form 'ein', we can create a new reading with the correct tags belonging to that form:

```
COPY (m SUGGEST) EXCEPT (nt)
 TARGET (&det-n-nt/m-agr) ;
```

The special tag `SUGGEST` indicates to `divvun-suggest` that this is a suggestion; given the right lemma and tags, the morphological generator will give the correct form for readings tagged `SUGGEST`. With this in place, the user will also see a drop-down with the suggestion 'ein'.

We may also want to extend the underline to the noun, to indicate the relevant context of the error. We do this by adding a relation `RIGHT` to the noun:

```
ADDRELATION (RIGHT) (&det-n-nt/m-agr)
 TO (1 (n)) ;
```

This will both extend the underline to include the noun, and ensure suggestions will include the noun, so *'eit rekneskap' gets the suggestion 'ein rekneskap'.

The relation is called `RIGHT` since we're extending the right-hand end of the underline. We can also add a `LEFT` relation if we want to extend the underline to the left of the main error cohort (the word with the `&` tag).

Plug-ins may show helpful explanations for why something is considered an error. These explanations are written in the file `errors.xml`, and may refer to word of the main error cohort with the string `$1` – the module `divvun-suggest` will replace `$1` with the corresponding word form (here 'eit'). To refer to another word in an explanation, we can add the $2 (or $3 etc.) relation to it in the same way as RIGHT, and then use $2 in the XML description (which here would be replaced with 'rekneskap'), turning a template message like `'$1' is neuter, but '$2' is masculine` into *'eit' is neuter, but 'rekneskap' is masculine* in the plugin.

5 Adding particles in Lule Sámi

Some times we need to add new words in corrections, for example missing particles:

(3) *Boahtá sån sijddaj?
come.PRS.3SG PRON.3SG siida.ILL

(4) Boahtá gus sån
come.PRS.3SG PCLE.QST PRON.3SG
sijddaj?
siida.ILL
'Is s/he coming home?'

To achieve this, we use the regular CG feature ADDCOHORT, along with a tag &ADDED to signify to divvun-suggest that this cohort did not exist in the input. Since the word did not exist in the input, we put the error tag on the preceding word, and give that a relation RIGHT to the added word.[5] The user will then see a correction from 'Boahtá' to 'Boahtá gus'.

6 Linking errors to each other in Irish

Errors may be spread across several words that need to be fixed as one. We may have a lone noun with the wrong case, but if it has an article in front, both may be wrong and need to be fixed.

Consider the Irish phrase below, where (5) has two words that need changing, example (6) being the correction:

(5) *Parlaimint **an Eoraip**
Parliament the.SG.DEF Europe.FEM.COM.SG

(6) Parlaimint **na hEorpa**
Parliament the.GEN.SG.DEF.FEM

Europe.FEM.GEN.SG.DEFART
'Parliament of Europe'

Here we want our suggestion to include changes to both the noun and the article as in Figure 5. (As the screenshot shows, the missing human-readable error explanation becomes glaringly obvious when testing in a plug-in UI.)

[5]The added word should also get the same error tag, in case there are several possible errors in the context.

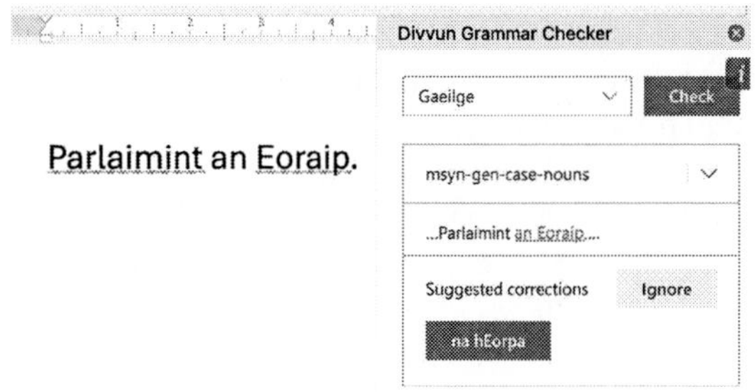

Figure 5: Divvun Grammar checking for Irish (Microsoft by default shows the red underlines of English grammar checking).

The below rules will correct the noun:

```
ADD (&msyn-gen-case-nouns)
 TARGET (Noun Com)
 IF (*-1 (Noun Com) BARRIER (*) - Art) ;


COPY (Gen Sg DefArt SUGGEST)
 EXCEPT (Com Sg &msyn-gen-case-nouns)
 TARGET (Com Sg &msyn-gen-case-nouns)
 IF (-1 (Art Def)) (NEGATE 0 DefArt);
```

But we also want to correct its possible determiner. We could add the below rules, which will underline the determiner (in this context) and give it a suggestion:

```
ADD (&msyn-gen-case-nouns)
 TARGET ("an" Art Sg Def)
 IF (NEGATE 0 Gen)
    (1 (Noun &msyn-gen-case-nouns)) ;

COPY ("na" Gen Sg Def Fem SUGGEST)
 EXCEPT ("an" Sg Def &msyn-gen-case-nouns)
 TARGET (Art &msyn-gen-case-nouns)
 IF (1 (Noun Fem)) ;
```

However, with these rules alone, the system will see two separate, independent errors, leading to two disconnected underlines, each with their suggestion. This is not ideal. We want the user to be able to pick both corrections at once, since they belong together. To tie them together, we (somewhat arbitrarily) call the noun the "main" word of the error complex, and add a LEFT relation from the noun to the determiner:

```
ADDRELATION ($2 LEFT) (&msyn-gen-case-nouns)
 TO (-1 (Art &msyn-gen-case-nouns)) ;
```

We use the term *co-errors* for any words of the error complex that we do not identify as the *main* error cohort. The difference between main and co-errors *may* coincide with syntactic relations, but does not need to – the main error word is often chosen by the grammar writer based on what is most stably wrong in this type of error.

Strictly speaking, we do not need an error tag at all for the article in this case. However, as we shall see below there may be several competing ways of correcting a complex error, and so we need to tell the system that *this* correction of the article belongs with *this* correction of the noun. We use relations to tie together the cohorts, but relations are cohort-to-cohort, not reading-to-reading. So we need a matching error tag[6] as well to pick out which *readings* of the two cohorts are connected.

7 Suggesting several things for one error in Lule Sámi numeral phrases

Numeral phrases are complex in Lule Sámi and they can be long. They typically consist of at minimum a numeral and a noun with possible modifiers (attributive adjectives or nouns in genitive case to mark the possessor). However, they can also contain coordinated numerals, demonstratives in front of the numeral and coordinated nouns.

(7) *Moadda tjijnnujn, girkkojn
some.ACC.SG cinema.INE.PL, church.INE.PL
ja almulasj bájkijn li dákkár
and common place.INE.PL are these
teleslivŋŋasa.
hearing.loop

(8) Moatten tjijnnun, girkkon
some.INE.SG cinema.INE.SG, church.INE.SG
ja almulasj bájken li dákkár
and common.ATTR place.INE.SG are these
teleslivŋŋasa.
hearing.loop
'Such audio induction loops are found in many cinemas, churches and public places'

We would like it to be corrected as displayed in Figure 6.

Ex. (8) consists of the following components:

There can be errors in only the demonstrative, only the numeral, only the noun, or in all three parts. That also means that sometimes we have several suggestions for corrections, depending on if we want to adapt the numeral to the noun, or

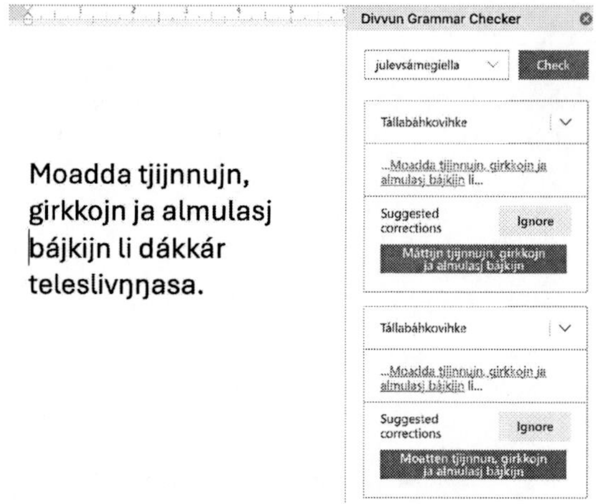

Figure 6: Divvun Grammar checking for Lule Sámi

the noun to the numeral. Technically that requires that we link all parts together in a certain way and also the corrections. In this case, we have an alternative correction which must be kept separate – all rules for the example (8) correction use the tag `&msyn-numphrase-sgine` while those for example (9) use the tag `&msyn-numphrase-sgcom` in order to avoid interference.

(9) Måttijn tjijnnujn,
some.COM.SG ccomma.COM.SG,
girkkojn ja almulasj
church.COM.SG and common.ATTR
bájkijn
place.COM.SG

The main error here is the first noun after the numeral, *tjijnnujn*. The numeral needs the coerrortag, and so do all the coordinated nouns. That means we need `LEFT` and `RIGHT` relations; `RIGHT` relations to the coordinated things to the right of the main error, and `LEFT` relations to the left of the main error, i.e. the numeral and/or the demonstrative.

1. ADD-rules for nouns
   (a) main error
   (b) coordinated nouns (co-error to the right)
   (c) coordinated nominal modifiers
2. COPY rules for nouns

[6] In some rules you will see the error tag with a prefix **co&**, like `co&syn-abs-wordorder`; this is equivalent to `&syn-abs-wordorder`, except it makes it explicit that this cohort is not the "main" word of the error, so for example it should not be `$1` in explanations.

3. ADD-rules for simple and coordinated numerals (co-errors)

4. ADDRELATION-rules from the main error to its co-errors

   (a) main noun to first coordinated noun (RIGHT)

   (b) main noun to second coordinated nouns (RIGHT)

   (c) noun to numeral (LEFT)

5. COPY rules for numerals

6. ADD-rule for demonstratives

7. ADDRELATION rules for demonstratives (LEFT)

8. COPY rule for demonstratives

In addition to the RIGHT and LEFT relation we add $2–$N to each of the co-errors (the main error being by default associated with $1), so we can refer to the word forms in the explanation shown in the MS Word plug-in etc.

8 Changing word order in Greenlandic

Word order rules are often relevant for languages that have a different standard word order than the languages they compete with, such as minority languages that are spoken in a majority language context. Both Greenlandic and Lule Sámi have SOV (subject object verb) as their standard word orders, whereas their competitors Danish, Swedish and Norwegian have a SVO standard word order, which may interfere and lead to word order errors. Danish and Greenlandic also differ in terms of noun phrase internal structure.

Moving around parts of the sentences requires that we know where the part has been before and at the same time know where we want to move it to.

The following set of rules for Greenlandic applies to possessive nominal phrases that are marked for their possessor, which is in relative case. The rules add an error-tag to a noun in absolutive case (the head of a possessum) preceded by an adjectival absolutive and a noun in relative case (the possessor). This is an error since in Greenlandic, possessor noun phrases place the adjective after and not before noun. We also add the DELETE tag since it is to be removed in the suggestion. We then copy the respective cohort (that belongs to the possessive adjectival noun phrase) and place it in the desired position (without removing the one in the erroneous position) and mark it with the tag &ADDED to show that this is not the original but the corrected position. Lastly, we establish a relation from the erroneous one so that we get the correct underline.

```
WITH (N Abs) + $$NUMERUS - ADJEKTIVISK IF
    (*-1 (3SgPoss Abs) + $$NUMERUS + ADJEKTIVISK
        BARRIER (*) - Abs
        LINK *-1 BOS LINK 1 (N Rel Sg))     # _C1_
    (NEGATE *0 &msyn-obj-marking-abs-3PlO) # _C2_
    (NEGATE 0  &msyn-obj-marking-abs-3PlO) # _C3_
{
  ADD (&syn-abs-wordorder DELETE) (*);
  COPYCOHORT
    (&ADDED co&syn-abs-wordorder)       # new tags
    EXCEPT (DELETE &syn-abs-wordorder) # remove these
    TARGET    (*)        # Copy from main WITH target
    TO BEFORE (jC1 (*)) # Put it before _C1_ context
    ;
  ADDRELATION ($3 LEFT) (*)
     TO (jC1 (*) LINK -1 (&ADDED));
};
```

This rule-set uses the new WITH (Swanson et al., 2023) feature in CG – the rules inside the braces will only apply when the outer context conditions match. Their target is the first context, and they may refer to the following outer contexts with C1, C2 and so on. This feature lets us avoid some redundancy in rule contexts.

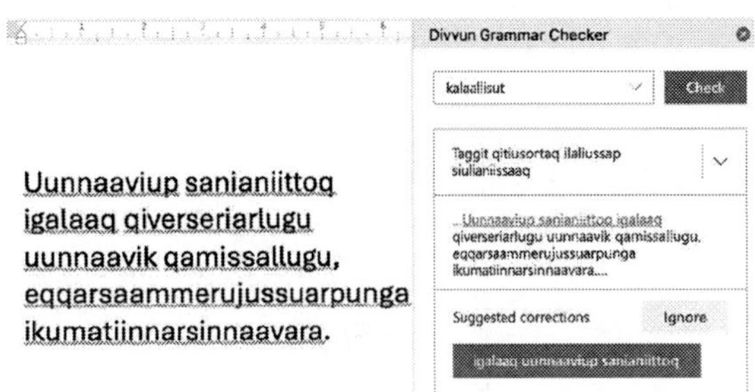

Figure 7: Divvun Grammar checking for Greenlandic (with MS Word default English spellchecking)

Example (10) has the wrong word order; the correct order is in example (11).[7]

(10) **Uunnaaviup saniani ittoq**
kettle.REL.SG next.to.3SGPOSS.ABS.SG
igalaaq qiverseriarlugu
window.ABS.SG upon.opening.1SG>3SG

[7]For further analysis check https://nutserut.gl/gloss.

uunnaavik
kettle.ABS.SG
qamissallugu,
when.intend.to.turn.off.1SG>3SG
eqqarsaammerujussuarpunga
think.suddenly.1SG
ikumatiinnarsinnaavara.
can.leave.on.1SG>3SG
'After/upon opening the window (which is) next to the kettle, when I went to turn off the kettle I suddenly thought I can leave it on.'

(11) **Igalaaq uunnaaviup sanianiittoq** qiverseriarlugu uunnaavik qamissallugu, eqqarsaammerujussuarpunga ikumatiinnarsinnaavara.

The word error correction is shown in Figure 7.

9 Performance

The Divvun grammar checker system is used for many languages, some with more extensive support than others. Mikkelsen and Wiechetek (2023) contains an evaluation of the state of the first version of the Lule Sámi grammar checker. That analysis does not include the new developments for multiword support. An extensive evaluation is out of scope of this paper, but we plan on evaluating, both the updated Lule Sámi system as well as other languages involved in the future.

Preliminary results for Lule Sámi numeral phrases are promising, cf. Table 1. We tested on the 39,891 word Lule Sámi corpus for evaluation purposes (SIKOR), which has been marked-up and then run through *GramDivvun*.

Metric	Count
False Positives	12
False Negatives	17
True Positives	42
F_1	74.3 %

Table 1: Evaluation results for numeral phrases

A third of the false negatives in our test are numeral phrases including the word *åvtå/avta*. We decided against performing grammar checking on this word due to its polysemy (in addition to the numeral *one* it also means *same*) which would lead to a lot of false positives.

Some of the false positives regard other grammatical constructions like *20 jahkásasj* meaning *20-year-old* and are mistaken to be part of a larger numeral phrase by the grammar checker.

10 Summing up

As this paper shows, the combination of finite state morphologies and Constraint Grammar lets us detect and correct a wide range of complex grammatical errors in morphologically rich, low-resource languages. The rule formalism and the surrounding tools enable proofing for languages that do not have official support in word processors like Microsoft Word and Google Docs – and in principle any text editing tool with some support for spelling and grammar plug-ins. Bridging the gap from the command-line to mainstream user interfaces both increases the usefulness of these tools, and boosts development progress – the user interface lets the linguist see the feedback from new angles and highlights shortcomings one might otherwise miss. When working on different languages, we discover new challenges in error correction. Looking forward, we plan to explore additional languages, cover more error types and streamline the rule writing process. The approach described in this paper demonstrates that rule-based GEC is an effective solution for correcting complex errors in languages that receive little-to-no official support from mainstream software vendors, enabling a user-friendly interface which gives speakers and learners of low-resource languages access to high quality proofing tools.

Acknowledgments

We thank Inga Lill Sigga Mikkelsen for her invaluable work on Lule Sámi, her help with the evaluation and suggestions for how the Constraint Grammar formalism should practically resolve grammar checking corrections. We thank Judithe Denbæk for her work on Greenlandic grammar checking. We thank Seanán Ó Coistín for his initiative to start up Irish grammar checking.

References

Antti Arppe. 2000. Developing a grammar checker for Swedish. In *Proceedings of the 12th Nordic Conference of Computational Linguistics (NoDaLiDa 1999)*, pages 13–27, Department of Linguistics, Norwegian University of Science and Technology (NTNU), Trondheim, Norway.

Kenneth R Beesley and Lauri Karttunen. 2003. Finite-state morphology: Xerox tools and techniques. *CSLI, Stanford*, pages 359–375.

Eckhard Bick. 2000. *The Parsing System 'Palavras': Automatic Grammatical Analysis of Portuguese in a Constraint Grammar Framework (higher doctoral dissertation)*. Aarhus University Press, Aarhus.

Eckhard Bick. 2015. DanProof: Pedagogical spell and grammar checking for Danish. In *Proceedings of the 10th International Conference Recent Advances in Natural Language Processing (RANLP 2015)*, pages 55–62, Hissar, Bulgaria. INCOMA Ltd.

Eckhard Bick and Tino Didriksen. 2015. CG-3 – beyond classical Constraint Grammar. In *Proceedings of the 20th Nordic Conference of Computational Linguistics (NoDaLiDa 2015)*, pages 31–39. Linköping University Electronic Press, Linköpings universitet.

Tino Didriksen. 2010. *Constraint Grammar Manual: 3rd version of the CG formalism variant*. GrammarSoft ApS, Denmark.

Vsevolod Dyomkin. 2015. Running lisp in production.

Fred Karlsson. 1990a. Constraint Grammar as a Framework for Parsing Running Text. In *Proceedings of the 13th Conference on Computational Linguistics (COLING 1990)*, volume 3, pages 168–173, Helsinki, Finland. Association for Computational Linguistics.

Fred Karlsson. 1990b. Constraint grammar as a framework for parsing unrestricted text. In *Proceedings of the 13th International Conference of Computational Linguistics*, volume 3, pages 168–173, Helsinki.

Fred Karlsson, Atro Voutilainen, Juha Heikkilä, and Arto Anttila. 1995. *Constraint Grammar: A Language-Independent System for Parsing Unrestricted Text*. Mouton de Gruyter, Berlin.

Krister Lindén, Erik Axelson, Senka Drobac, Sam Hardwick, Juha Kuokkala, Jyrki Niemi, Tommi A Pirinen, and Miikka Silfverberg. 2013. Hfst—a system for creating nlp tools. In *International workshop on systems and frameworks for computational morphology*, pages 53–71. Springer.

Inga Lill Sigga Mikkelsen and Linda Wiechetek. 2023. Supporting language users-releasing a full-fledged lule sámi grammar checker. In *Proceedings of the NoDaLiDa 2023 Workshop on Constraint Grammar-Methods, Tools and Applications*, pages 37–45.

SIKOR. UiT The Arctic University of Norway and the Norwegian Saami Parliament's Saami text collection, Version 06.11.2018. `http://gtweb.uit.no/korp`. Accessed: 2018-11-06.

Daniel Swanson, Tino Didriksen, and Francis Tyers. 2023. With context: Adding rule-grouping to visl cg-3. In *Proceedings of the NoDaLiDa 2023 Workshop on Constraint Grammar-Methods, Tools and Applications*, pages 10–14.

Linda Wiechetek, Katri Hiovain-Asikainen, Inga Lill Sigga Mikkelsen, Sjur Moshagen, Flammie Pirinen, Trond Trosterud, and Børre Gaup. 2022. Unmasking the myth of effortless big data - making an open source multi-lingual infrastructure and building language resources from scratch. In *Proceedings of the Thirteenth Language Resources and Evaluation Conference*, pages 1167–1177, Marseille, France. European Language Resources Association.

Linda Wiechetek, Sjur Nørstebø Moshagen, and Kevin Brubeck Unhammer. 2019. Seeing more than whitespace — tokenisation and disambiguation in a North Sámi grammar checker. In *Proceedings of the 3rd Workshop on the Use of Computational Methods in the Study of Endangered Languages Volume 1 (Papers)*, pages 46–55, Honolulu. Association for Computational Linguistics.

Towards Natural Language Explanations of Constraint Grammar Rules

Daniel Swanson
Indiana University
Department of Linguistics
Bloomington, Indiana
dangswan@iu.edu

Abstract

This paper presents a general-purpose parser for static analysis of Constraint Grammar rules (that is, examining only the rules, not potential inputs and outputs) and applies it to the task of translating rules into comprehensible explanations of behavior. An interactive interface for exploring how individual components of each rule contribute to these translations is also presented.

1 Introduction

Constraint Grammar (Karlsson et al., 2011; Bick and Didriksen, 2015) is a rule-based procedural text processing paradigm which can be used for a wide range of tasks, from part-of-speech tagging to word sense disambiguation to parsing to translation. The formalism for expressing these rules is quite compact, and can, at times, give rise to extremely complicated and arcane rules. Deciphering what such rules do can often be rather challenging, particularly for beginners.

For example, consider the rule in Figure 1 from the parser in Swanson and Tyers (2022). The grammar operates on a corpus which has been tagged for some syntactic relations but does not have full trees. This particular rule tries to attach a clause root to an immediately preceding clause root that is a verb of speaking and is not as deeply nested in quotations. For example, given the input "He said 'Go.'.", the word "said" would have `<txt:0>`, indicating that it was not a quotation and "go" would have `<txt:1>`, indicating that it was one quote deep and the rule would make "go" a child of "said".

This rule occurs in a collection of roughly 20 others with no comments other than the section heading "Clause Connections" for context. Ideally, any nontrivial rule would be accompanied by an explanatory comment to aid in deciphering it, but this is often not the case, leaving a daunting task for those who might later seek to understand a grammar.

To aid in remedying this problem, we now present an interactive tool which translates Constraint Grammar rules into English sentences and highlights which piece of the rule contributes each piece of the explanation, which can serve as a starting point for documenting existing grammars in addition to providing support to students trying to learn Constraint Grammar.

The paper is organized as follows: Section 2 describes our CG parser, Section 3 describes our translation rules, Section 4 describes the interactive interface for these translations, and Section 5 concludes.

2 Parsing Constraint Grammar

In order to explain a rule, it is first necessary to parse the rule. For this task, we employ the Tree-Sitter library (Brunsfeld et al., 2024). Tree-Sitter provides tooling for writing context-free grammars which compile to efficient parsers with bindings in many major programming languages. The original purpose of the library was as an alternative to regular expressions for syntax highlighting. As a result, it is fast and robust against incomplete or invalid input, which allows our tool to produce useful output even if the user pastes in an invalid rule. It also supports incremental re-parsing after edits, though we do not yet make use of this feature.

An example of a rule in the grammar definition is shown in Figure 2. This rule describes how to parse a tag list, which consists of the `LIST` keyword, a set name, an equals sign, a sequence of tags, and a semicolon. It labels the name and the list of tags, so that processing scripts can more easily retrieve those. These rules are semantically similar to other parser generators, such as

Proceedings of the 9th Workshop on Constraint Grammar and Finite State NLP, pages 28–31
March 5, 2025

```
SET NonPredAdv = (advb) - (role:P) ;
SET Top = (_) - (conj) - (@discourse) - NonPredAdv ;
WITH Top + (/^<txt:\(\\d+\)>$/r)
  IF (-1* Top + (VSTR:<txt<$1>) BARRIER Top) {
    SETPARENT (*) TO (jC1 (*)) ;
    MAP (@ccomp) (*) IF (jC1 SpeakingVerb) ;
    MAP (@xcomp) (verb infc) IF (jC1 XcompInf) (c (prep)) ;
} ;
```

Figure 1: A compound rule (Swanson et al., 2023) from the parser in Swanson and Tyers (2022) which attaches clause roots to the corresponding speaking verb. The set SpeakingVerb is a list of lemmas of verbs which can introduce quotations and the set XcompInf is a list of control verbs that take infinitive complements. Tags prefixed with @ are dependency labels and the rest are part-of-speech tags, apart from role:P, which indicates that the source data marks the word as a predicate, _, which indicates that the source data marks the word as the root of an independent clause, and <txt:N>, which indicates that a segment of text is N layers of quotation deep (so <txt:0> is narrative and <txt:2> is a quotation within a quotation).

```
LIST: $ => kwd('LIST'),
list: $ => seq(
  $.LIST,
  field('name', $.setname),
  choice($.eq, $.pluseq),
  field('value', $.taglist),
  $.semicolon,
),
```

Figure 2: A Tree-Sitter rule for parsing LIST definitions. A list node is defined as consisting of a LIST keyword, a name, an operator, a list of tags, and a semicolon.

YACC (Levine et al., 1992), though expressed in JavaScript syntax. The present CG parser consists of 101 such rules and has been tested against every CG file maintained by the Apertium project (Forcada et al., 2011; Khanna et al., 2021).

An example of the output of this rule is shown in Figure 3. Given the list of gender tags shown, the overall parser will produce the tree. This is the default string representation of the trees, with nodes denoted by S-expressions and field names indicated by colons. For example, (tag (ntag)) indicates an ntag node[1] which is a child of a tag node.

The parser is usable for static analysis and syntax highlighting and is available from GitHub[2],

Input:

```
LIST Gender = m f nt ;
```

Output:

```
(source_file
  (list
    (LIST)
    name: (setname)
    (eq)
    value: (taglist
      (tag (ntag))
      (tag (ntag))
      (tag (ntag)))
    (semicolon)))
```

Figure 3: The parse tree of a CG declaration as produced by the Tree-Sitter grammar.

NPM[3], and PyPI[4].

3 Translation Rules

In order to generate the English translation of a given tree, we apply a set of rules that extract a node and its descendants using Tree-Sitter's builtin query system and map them to string templates which those descendants are inserted into. For example, the template for a setname node is the set {name}, where name is the name of the set as it appears in the rule. Rules are applied

[1] ntag is a non-quoted tag, contrasted with qtag, which is a quoted tag.

[2] https://github.com/apertium/tree-sitter-apertium

[3] https://www.npmjs.com/package/tree-sitter-cg

[4] https://pypi.org/project/tree-sitter-cg/

Define the set NonPredAdv as any word which has the tag advb and does not have the tag role:P.

Define the set Top as any word which has the tag _ and does not have the tag conj and does not have the tag @discourse and does not match the set NonPredAdv.

Find a word which matches the set Top and has the tag /^<txt:\(\\d+\)>$/r *in context some reading in the cohort 1 positions to the left or further in that direction (stop looking if you reach one which matches the set Top) is one which matches the set Top and has the tag* VSTR:<txt<$1> *and run the following rules:*

> *Set the parent of any word which is the target of the containing WITH rule to some reading in the cohort found by context test 1 in the containing WITH rule which must be one which can be any word.*
>
> *If some reading in the cohort found by context test 1 in the containing WITH rule is one which matches the set SpeakingVerb then add the tag @ccomp to a word which is the target of the containing WITH rule and prevent other rules from adding tags.*
>
> *If some reading in the cohort found by context test 1 in the containing WITH rule is one which matches the set XcompInf and some reading in a child cohort is one which has the tag prep then add the tag @xcomp to a word the tags verb, infc and prevent other rules from adding tags.*

Figure 4: The output of the translator for the rule shown in Figure 1.

in order and from top to bottom of the tree, with the first to match taking precedence.

Most of the rules are written to capture a single node and translate it without knowing what its parent or child is. Thus an `inlineset` node, which can be a setname or a list of tags in parentheses or various combinations of the two, is translated using `which has ...` or `which matches ...` and most other nodes which might contain `inlinesets` are written to ensure that that makes grammatical sense. Occasionally, this is not feasible and in those cases, a rule can be written which captures its grandchildren or is conditioned on its parent. An example of the former is a special case of the `inlineset` rule which checks for an inline set that only contains the tag `*` and translates it to `any word`. An example of the latter is a special case of that which further checks if the set is the target of a rule inside a `WITH` block, in which case the translation is `the target of the containing WITH rule`. An example of the output of the translator is shown in Figure 4.

We have implemented processors for these rules in both Python and JavaScript, enabling usage in both offline scripts and the browser.

4 Interactive Interface

We have created an online front-end for the translation rules[5]. The interface presents two panes. The user can type or paste rules in the left pane and the right pane will show a live-updating translation of the rules. A screenshot of the interface is shown in Figure 5.

We use the Tree-Sitter parse tree to provide syntax highlighting to the rules in the left pane. In addition, we tag each node of the tree in both the source rules and the translation, so that if the user hovers over either side, the corresponding text in the other pane is highlighted.

5 Conclusion and Future Work

In this paper, we have presented a general-purpose parser for static analysis of Constraint Grammar rules, as well as a system on top of that for translating those rules into English sentences.

The biggest limitation of the current system is that the parser does not distinguish between different types of tags, so simple tags like `n`, regular expressions like `/n\(\\d\)/r`, string substitutions like `VSTR:$1`, and numeric comparisons like <P>3> are all currently parsed as simply unquoted tags, making it difficult to fully translate them based solely on the parse tree. Thus in the translation in Figure 4, there is no indication of the fact that the `WITH` condition is looking for a pair of words where one has a numeric <txt> tag with a lower value than the other. Unfortunately, it is probably impossible to solve this problem completely, since string substitution can generate special tags, and thus some thing cannot be identi-

[5] Available at https://mr-martian.github.io/rule-explainer/

Left Pane:

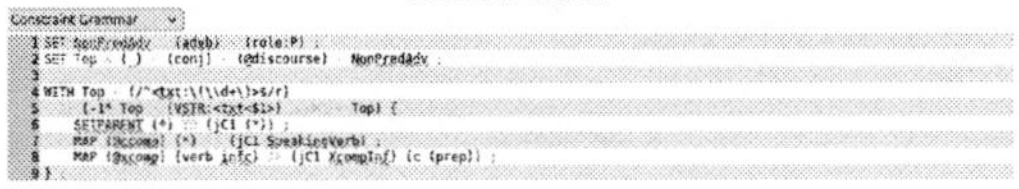

Right Pane:

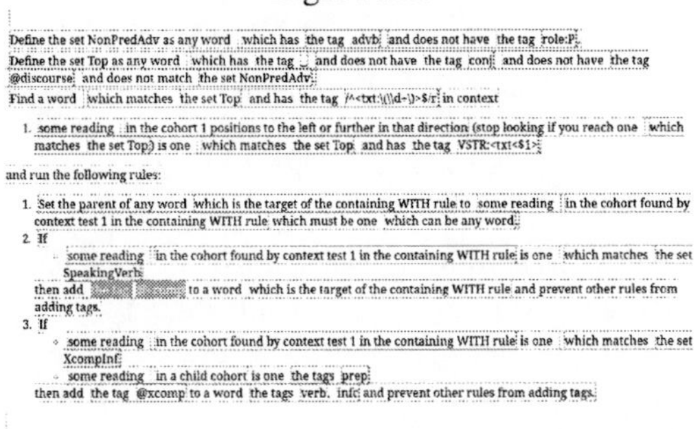

Figure 5: The interactive interface for the rule-explainer. The user is hovering over the words *the tag @ccomp* in the right-hand pane and so the `@ccomp` tag on line 7 is highlighted in the left-hand pane. (In a webbrowser, these sections will appear next to each other, but here they are shown vertically for the sake of legibility.)

fied without executing the rule, but some amount of greater specificity is probably possible.

Another avenue for expansion is to translate into other natural languages or into multiple levels of detail (that is, to collapse some parts of the explanation if they are not needed). Perhaps there could be a more beginner-friendly set of rules that explain each step at length and a more simple version for users who understand CG rules in general and just happen to be confused by one in particular.

Finally, one could imagine a system that does the reverse of this one and translates English descriptions into actual CG rules, along the lines of what Tyers and Howell (2021) report doing manually. This system could be used to generate an initial parallel corpus for training a reverse system and also to help users double check the output.

Acknowledgments

I would like to thank Tino Didriksen for his assistance in the development and packaging of the Tree-Sitter grammar. I would like to thank Matthew Fort and Meesum Alam for their feedback on the structure of some of the rule descriptions. Finally, I would like to thank Robert Pugh, Nils Hjortnaes, and Francis Tyers for their comments on earlier drafts of this paper.

References

Eckhard Bick and Tino Didriksen. 2015. CG-3 — beyond classical constraint grammar. In *Proceedings of the 20th Nordic Conference of Computational Linguistics (NODALIDA 2015)*, pages 31–39, Vilnius, Lithuania. Linköping University Electronic Press, Sweden.

Max Brunsfeld, Amaan Qureshi, Andrew Hlynskyi, Patrick Thomson, ObserverOfTime, Josh Vera, dundargoc, Phil Turnbull, Timothy Clem, Douglas Creager, Andrew Helwer, Rob Rix, Daumantas Kavolis, Hendrik van Antwerpen, Michael Davis, Will Lillis, Ika, Amin Yahyaabadi, Tuan-Ahn Nguyen, bfredl, Matt Massicotte, Stafford Brunk, Christian Clason, Niranjan Hasabnis, Mingkai Dong, Samuel Moelius, Steven Kalt, Segev Finer, and Kolja. 2024. tree-sitter/tree-sitter: v0.24.4.

Mikel L Forcada, Mireia Ginestí-Rosell, Jacob Nordfalk, Jim O'Regan, Sergio Ortiz-Rojas, Juan Antonio Pérez-Ortiz, Felipe Sánchez-Martínez, Gema Ramírez-Sánchez, and Francis M Tyers. 2011. Apertium: a free/open-source platform for rule-based machine translation. *Machine translation*, 25:127–144.

Fred Karlsson, Atro Voutilainen, Juha Heikkilae, and Arto Anttila. 2011. *Constraint Grammar: a language-independent system for parsing unrestricted text*, volume 4. Walter de Gruyter.

Tanmai Khanna, Jonathan N Washington, Francis M Tyers, Sevilay Bayatlı, Daniel G Swanson, Tommi A Pirinen, Irene Tang, and Hector Alos i Font. 2021. Recent advances in apertium, a free/open-source rule-based machine translation platform for low-resource languages. *Machine Translation*, 35(4):475–502.

John R Levine, Tony Mason, and Doug Brown. 1992. *Lex & yacc*. O'Reilly Media, Inc.

Daniel Swanson, Tino Didriksen, and Francis M. Tyers. 2023. WITH context: Adding rule-grouping to VISL CG-3. In *Proceedings of the NoDaLiDa 2023 Workshop on Constraint Grammar - Methods, Tools and Applications*, pages 10–14, Tórshavn, Faroe Islands. Association of Computational Linguistics.

Daniel Swanson and Francis Tyers. 2022. A Universal Dependencies treebank of Ancient Hebrew. In *Proceedings of the Thirteenth Language Resources and Evaluation Conference*, pages 2353–2361, Marseille, France. European Language Resources Association.

Francis M Tyers and Nick Howell. 2021. Morphological analysis and disambiguation for breton. *Language Resources and Evaluation*, 55(2):431–473.

A Mansi FST and spellchecker

Csilla Horváth
Helsinki University
csilla.horvath@helsinki.fi

Jack Rueter
Helsinki University
jack.rueter@helsinki.fi

Trond Trosterud
UiT The Arctic University of Norway
trond.trosterud@uit.no

Abstract

The article presents a finite state transducer and spellchecker for Mansi, an Ob-Ugric Uralic language spoken in northwestern Siberia. Mansi has a rich but mostly agglutinative morphology, with a morphophonology dominated by sandhi phenomena. With a small set of morphophonological rules (32 twolc rules) and a lexicon consisting of 12,000 Mansi entries and a larger set of propernouns we were able to build a transducer covering 98.9 % of a large (700k) newspaper corpus. Being a part of the GiellaLT infrastructure, the transducer was turned into a spellchecker. The most common spelling error in Mansi is the omission of length marks on vowels, and for the 1000 most common words containing long vowels, the spellchecker was able to give a correct suggestion as top-five in 98.3 % of the cases, and as first suggestion in 91.3 % of the cases.

1 Introduction

The article presents a finite state transducer and spellchecker for Mansi. Section 2 presents the Mansi language, its orthography and its grammar. Section 3 is the main part of the article, it presents the Mansi grammatacial model, discusses how it was made, and gives an evaluation of its performance. Section 4 presents and evaluates the Mansi spellchecker. Finally comes a conclusion.

2 Background

2.1 The Mansi language in society

Mansi is a severely endangered minority language, spoken mainly by the Mansi, an indigenous people of the Russian North. Genetically, it belongs to the Ob-Ugric branch of the Uralic language family. According to the latest Russian census data, approximately 1,000 people claimed to use the Mansi language (Перепись, 2020a), the vast majority of speakers reside on the territory of the Khanty-Mansi Automous Okrug - Yugra and the Sverdlovsk Oblast (cf. Перепись (2020b)). Four Mansi dialect groups were documented in the nineteenth century, each of which had several subdialects. While other dialect groups have become moribund, then extinct during the 20th century, varieties of the Northern Mansi dialect group are still in use, both in spoken and written form (cf. Virtanen and Horváth (2023)). The Mansi literary standard is based on the Sosva variety of Northern Mansi.

Regarding the status of the language, Mansi is an indigenous minoritised language spoken in Western Siberia, it has no official status, not at the regional nor at the municipal level. Mansi plays a minor role in its Russian-dominated, multi-ethnic and multilingual environment. Its situation is heavily affected by the loss of the traditional way of life and by rapid urbanisation. Mansi is barely present in official or semi-official domains, such as legislation, public transport or street signage, and due to its low economic significance, Mansi is also absent from the business sphere and only plays a marginal role in the labour market. Nowadays, Mansi has its strongest position in the sphere of family language use, but since the turn of the century it has been introduced to new domains of language use as well, such as heritage language education, theatre and popular music, print, broadcast and social media (c.f. Horváth (2020, 2024, 2025, forthcoming)).

2.2 The development of the Mansi orthography

The Mansi language, in a way similar to that of other indigenous languages of the Russian North, has a history of literacy spanning almost a century. The first publications appeared in 1931, and

Proceedings of the 9th Workshop on Constraint Grammar and Finite State NLP, pages 32–37
March 5, 2025

originally Mansi was written in a Latin-based alphabet. This changed, however, with the transition to a Cyrillic-based alphabet in 1937 (Chernetsov, 1937, 168). Since 1937, the Mansi writing system has undergone minor changes. In the earliest period, the Cyrillic transcription contained no special characters, and vowel length was not marked either (as e.g. in Chernetsova (1938)). Later, a special character was introduced to denote the velar nasal (as e.g. in Balandin and Vakhrusheva (1972)), and vowel length has been marked with diacritics since the 1980s (as e.g. in Rombandeyeva et al. (1985). Currently, two slightly different variants of Mansi orthography are in use, one used in some of the academic and pedagogical publications (dictionaries, traditional schoolbooks), the other used in all other work, including print and broadcast media, social media, even schoolbooks designed for heritage language learners (Virtanen and Horváth, 2023, 667). For a more in-depth discussion of Mansi orthography, see Bradley and Skribnik (2021).

2.3 Mansi grammar

Mansi is a Uralic language, spoken mostly in Western Siberia. Typologically it forms a Sprachbund together with the neighbouring Khanty and Northern Samoyed languages, showing similar traits especially within the morphology, but also within syntax and morphophonology. It has a vowel system consisting of six vowels, each with a phonologically distinct short and long vowel, and an (only short) schwa. Mansi shows no vowel harmony and almost no vowel or consonant stem alternations. The morphophonological processes involved in Mansi inflection are mainly stem adjusting processes resulting from suffixes being attached to vowel or consonant stems.

Pronouns are inflected for 5 grammatical cases. The nouns have a six morphological (mainly adverbial) cases and a possessive declension. Verbs are inflected both for subject number and person and for object number, as well as for tense, mood and diathesis. Both nouns and verbs inflect for singular, dual and plural. There are also infinite forms, infinitive, gerund and participles.

Mansi is predominantly SOV, with adverbials allowed preverbally. The word order is not rigid, the verb may also be found sentence-initially in order to give it focus.

3 The Mansi Finite State Transducer

The Mansi grammatical analyser is made as two finite-state transducers, where the lower side of the *lexical* one corresponds to the upper side of the 74.40

The grammatical analyser is modeled in the GiellaLT infrastructure. For a presentation, see Moshagen et al. (2023).

3.1 Lexicon

At present, the Mansi grammatical model contains 825 continuation lexica and 12,063 stems with an additional set of over 145,000 shared lexemes at GiellaLT for the annotation of 100% equivalents of Russian names and toponyms (see Rueter, 2024).

The attestation of actual Mansi words required a consensus. On the basis of the word forms found in our newspaper corpus, we concluded that at least all words with Mansi morphology would be treated as Mansi words. One of the original issues had been that there was a large portion of the text in quotes, so it was difficult to establish which word forms were being used in context.

Despite previous work with the vocabulary, it soon became apparent that verbal conjugation and noun declension paradigms often had more than one variant per cell of morphological analysis. The Mansi word for 'house' *kol* has two forms to represent the singular nominative form with first person dual possessive marking, e.g., *колмēн*, *колмен*.

Even though many of the variations became apparent in short versus long vowels, there were also instances where verbs with <y> stems in the infinitive took <a> stem variants. We do not want overlapping paradigms with multiple identical forms, which would be the result of simply joining multiple paradigms for a single verb type. Since duplicate identical interpretation defeats the advantage of fostering rule-based concise morphology, we limit the description of additional paradigmatic cells to precise annotation where a descriptive analyser will identify any extra forms. Thus, our work continues here with designing optimal representations of verb and noun inflection types that avoid duplication of individual forms. This work is carried out with full-scale test paradigms for each individual inflection type.

3.2 Morphology

Mansi verbal morphology includes the detachment of prefixes from their verbal stems when negative particles are introduced with other possible particles. This entails the use of so-called flag diacritics, which are used in the description of languages with non-adjacent collocated morphology[1]

We use flag diacritics in the description of collective paired nouns in Mansi. Collective paired nouns tend to appear in combinations of kin terms. Such words are the equivalents of 'children' *āгит-пыгит* (lit. *girls-boys*) and 'my parents' *омагум-āтягум* (lit. my.mothers-my.fathers). In both instances, the first and second components take identical morphology, i.e., in the word for 'children' the word for 'girl' *āги* takes the nominative plural marker *т*, which is repeated on the word for 'boy' *пыг*. The flag diacritics disallow any analyses other than tandem, identical readings. The word for 'parents' is rendered according to the same requirements, but here 'mother' *ома* takes morphological marking for nominative dual with a first person singular possessor.

```
омагум-āтягум
ома+N+Du+Nom+PxSg1+Cmp/Coll+Err/Orth-no-hyphen
+Cmp#āтя+N+Du+Nom+PxSg1
```

The flag diacritics used in the description of verbs with detachable prefixes are used at two points in the continuation lexica. First, they are given with the entire lemma with correlation to the verb prefix in the stem, and they have a continuation lexicon to allow for work with orthography, i.e., hyphenation or not, and the possibility for negation. The next continuation lexicon then provides for joining the prefixes to individual stems. This is accomplished with a strategy involving diacritic flags based on the value of the individual prefixes, as there are fewer prefixes than main verbs.

3.3 Morphophonology

Morphophonological processes were treated in twolc, where initially stem-alternating processes are described according to the shape of the stem and the affixes. In order to take control of this variation, meta-symbols were added at the stem and affix boundary, partly also to the suffixes. The following rule deletes the initial suffix vowel *а/я* whenever the stem is marked with the %VO%: trigger.

```
"%{аяØ%}:0"
%{аяØ%}:0 <=> %{VO%}:  %> _  ;
```

[1]see, e.g., pair verbs in Komi-Zyrian Rueter et al., 2021, reduplication in Lushootseed Rueter et al., 2023.

Triggers are used to describe the stem-final phonology of a word and help in the realisation of desired changes in the stem and suffixes. In this manner, the designer can choose which spellings or misspellings are derived by using continuation lexicon strategies.

The traditional description of Mansi nouns divides them into five distinct groups (c.f. Riese (2001) and Rombandeeva (2017)). At a first glance, Mansi nouns look like they might be described as a single set of words. As newcomers to Mansi language description, however, we aligned our approach to what tradition dictated. The five stem types are divided according to the way they end: (1) stems ending in the vowel *i*; (2) stems ending in other vowels; (3) stems ending in one consonant, (4) stems ending in consonant clusters and (5) stems with syncope. Also, types 3, 4 and 5 have variation according to the palatalisation of the final consonant. This simple breakdown, in fact, is not the entire picture: Syncope only applies to the high non-labial vowel with a single following consonant. Phonologically, this vowel is a schwa, but in Mansi orthography it is written with either <ы> or <у>. The number of stem-final consonant may be directly related to the presence of a vowel at the onset of some suffixes, and palatal versus non-palatal is an important factor when considering the suffix onset. To this end, we placed morpheme boundary triggers describing the word-stem phonology. Not all patterns are consistent with usage, for example, there are two types of syncopating stems, one is soft *SYNCS* and the other is hard *SYNCH*, but there are also words that might fit the syncope patterns that do not syncopate. Here we use *NOSYNCS* and *NOSYNCH* triggers as distinct from *VCS* and *VCH*, so we will be able to develop the modelling needed in the generation and analysis of misspellings in the use of syncope.

At Giellalt, it is encouraged that code and strategies be reused where possible. In practice, this means that time can be saved by applying solutions already found and applied in other language projects. Thus, a meander occurred in the development of the verbal paradigm with regard to the tagging of third person object marking on verbs.

3.4 Building the transducer

Our team consisted of people with professional knowledge of the target language, vast experience in the implementation of finite-state description, testing, and spell checker development. This has meant that our contributions to the development of the analyser stem from complementary collaboration and the establishment of a mutual work flow. The language professional provides extensive paradigms for words in the language. The finite-state description is written by one researcher in constant consultation with the language professional and tester. The tester and spellchecking specialist leads the group, produces lists of lexemes not recognised by the analyser, and in collaboration with the other two workers helps to establish enhanced workflow strategies, such as having the language specialist make analysis notes for the lexemes misspelled most frequently. This is accomplished by remote meetings every other week, but it does not prevent the workers from contacting each other more often. Mansi native speakers assisted the team's work only occasionally, when explaining the unknown word forms, missing from the existing dictionaries.

Test paradigms are written for words representative of specific word classes. Nouns, for example, are divided according to traditional morphological descriptions, so that the resulting analysers can best fit the established norm. Since no one writes texts perfectly every time, and we hope the coding efforts will lead to invigoration in the language community with better perspectives in the future, we design the analyser so it will also recognise words regardless of their inconsistent spellings. In Northern Mansi, there are several factors contributing to misspelling. They stem from changes in the orthography involving the palatal *s*, an underdocumented use of long and short vowels, and multiple values for some cells in the paradigms. This is positive and means the orthography is still developing and will be for a number of decades to come. Our job is to make a description that allows writers and other language leeway.

Working as a group helps us to grow, especially, when we are trying to teach a new developer to become more self-sufficient, and when everyone is trying to keep language-independence at an optimal level. In Mansi, our solution for the orthographic representation is to use precomposed letters where-ever possible. This is due to the low development of UNICODE in the Cyrillic range, i.e., there are only two Cyrillic vowels precomposed with macrons. As such, we can only use the precomposed *ӯ* and *ӣ*, whereas the other long vowels are simply combinations with *U+0304*.

The absence of precomposed long vowels has meant that some corpus work and earlier code has been done using characters from the UNICODE Latin range (usually researchers), or non-UNICODE characters (media facilitators). To solve this problem, a keyboard specifically for Mansi that used precomposed Cyrillic-range characters where possible was built by Trond Trosterud. Our finite-state description of Mansi, as is the case with other languages, utilizes spell-relax strategies whereby Latin-range characters or non-standard character combinations can be recognized as their look-alike standard forms.

3.5 Evaluation

The development of the Mansi FST was done by testing against a newspaper corpus of 700000 words (Horváth et al., 2017). At present, the analyser recognises **98.86 %** of the words in the newspaper corpus. This impressive result is somewhat weakened by the fact that the analyser was developed on the same corpus. In contrast, however, words were added to the corpus based on their grammatical properties. Newspaper corpora, by their very nature, contain a vocabulary spanning many genres.

Proper nouns are a challenge for any language model. This grammatical model contains a language-independent set of 140000 names[2]. Restricting the test to words with initial capital letter (sentence-intitial words and names) weakens the coverage result from 98.86 % to 94.17 %. A weaker result is as expected, since names belong to an open category. Most of the missing words were either Russian words (Территории, 'territories', Утро, 'morning') or local names (Кантык-Ях).

Although our test corpus is both large (for an indigenous language) and representative for literary language use, it would no doubt have been relevant to test the speller against an unseen corpus. Unfortunately all available unseen text contained so much OCR errors that they made meaningful testing impossible.

4 Practical tools

The Mansi language model has been implemented as a spell checker, both online[3] and in Microsoft Word, 1.

[2] `https://github.com/giellalt/shared-urj-Cyrl/`

[3] https://divvun.org/proofing/online-speller.html

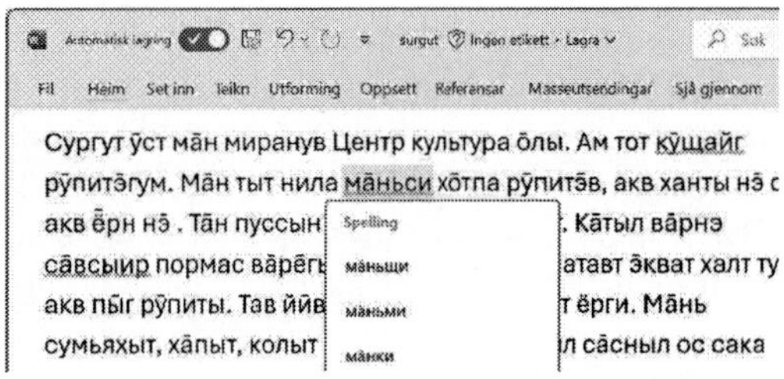

Figure 1: Mansi MS Word speller.

The overwhelmingly most common error in Mansi is use of the length mark for long vowels; the macron is often omitted where it should be or added where it does not belong. In order to test the spellchecker for its ability to correct length errors, we collected the words in the newspaper corpus containing long vowels, all in all 338937 words. In order to test the suggestion mechanism, we counted only the word forms that had an analysis, 12684 unique word forms. The long vowels were shortened, and pairs where shortening the vowel resulted in an existing word were removed. The resulting test suit contained 11064 word pairs. We tested both the full list and the list containing the 1000 most common long vowel words. The result is shown in table 1.

The result shows that the spellchecker is indeed capable of correcting this error type. Interestingly, the results from the most common words are better than for the whole material, this is probably because the rarer words were longer and therefore offered more possibilities for corrections.

Test	Words	1st pos	Top-5
Short-long	1000	91.30	98.30
Short-long	11064	86.77	96.72

Table 1: Testing error correction

5 Conclusion

Mansi is a language with a rich morphology but with relatively simple morphophonological processes. The main problem when modeling Mansi was to handle long-distance dependencies linked to prefixing, this was done with flag diacritics. As a result of this, a transducer with a relatively simple morphophonological component (32 rules) and a small lexicon (13.000 entries) and a large set of Russian and international names (145.000 entries) was able to give a text coverage above 98 %.

The transducer was turned into a spellchecker, and for the most common error type (omission of vowel length), it gave very good results, for the most common words 98.3 % of the suggestions were among the top-5 suggestions and 91.3 % were first suggestions. For other error types the results were not that good, here more work is needed.

Acknowledgments

Thanks to Sjur N. Moshagen for helping out with the implementation of the Mansi keyboard and proofing tools. Thanks to Mansi consultants for helping out with explaining unclear wordforms.

References

Aleksey Balandin and Matra Vakhrusheva. 1972. *Маньси букварь*. Просвещение, Ленинград.

Jeremy Bradley and Elena Skribnik. 2021. The many writing systems of Mansi: challenges in transcription and transliteration. In *Multilingual Facilitation*, pages 12–24.

Valeriy Chernetsov. 1937. Мансийский (вогульский) язык. In *Языки и письменность народов Севера I.*, pages 163–182, Москва, Ленинград. Государственное учебно-педагогическое издательство.

Irina Chernetsova. 1938. *Ловинтан магыс книга*. Государственное учебно-педагогическое издательство Наркромпроса, Ленинград.

Csilla Horváth. 2020. *The vitality and revitalisation attempts of the Mansi language in Khanty-Mansiysk*. Phd thesis, University of Szeged, Szeged.

Csilla Horváth. 2024. From the kitchen to pop culture: The role of Mansi heritage speakers in language shift and language revitalisation. *Faits de langues*, 54:197–212.

Csilla Horváth. 2025, forthcoming. The role of Ob-Ugric native speakers and heritage language speakers in creating Khanty and Mansi print, broadcast and social media. In *Minority Language Media*. Palgrave Macmillan.

Csilla Horváth, Norbert Szilágyi, Veronika Vincze, and Ágoston Nagy. 2017. Language technology resources and tools for Mansi: an overview. In *Proceedings of the 3rd International Workshop for Computational Linguistics of Uralic Languages*, pages 56–65, St. Petersburg, Russia. Association for Computational Linguistics.

Sjur Nørstebø Moshagen, Flammie Pirinen, Lene Antonsen, Børre Gaup, Inga Mikkelsen, Trond Trosterud, Linda Wiechetek, and Katri Hiovain-Asikainen. 2023. *The GiellaLT infrastructure: A multilingual infrastructure for rule-based NLP*, volume 2 of *NEALT Monograph Series*, pages 70–94. NEALT.

Timothy Riese. 2001. *Vogul*, volume 158 of *Languages of the world Materials*. Lincom Europa, München - Newcastle.

Evdokija Ivanovna Rombandeeva. 2017. *Современный мансийский язык: Лексика, фонетика, графика, орфография, морфология, словообразование*. Формат, Tymen.

Evkodiya Rombandeyeva, Matra Vakhrusheva, and Klavdiya Saynakhova. 1985. *Мāньси лāтынг*. Просвещение, Ленингад.

Jack Rueter. 2024. Testing and enhancement of language models (transducers) from GiellaLT (scientific blog).

Jack Rueter, Mika Hämäläinen, and Khalid Alnajjar. 2023. Modelling the reduplicating Lushootseed morphology with an FST and LSTM. In *Proceedings of the Workshop on Natural Language Processing for Indigenous Languages of the Americas (AmericasNLP)*, pages 40–46, Toronto, Canada. Association for Computational Linguistics.

Jack Rueter, Niko Partanen, Mika Hämäläinen, and Trond Trosterud. 2021. Overview of open-source morphology development for the Komi-Zyrian language: Past and future. In *Proceedings of the Seventh International Workshop on Computational Linguistics of Uralic Languages*, page 62–72, United States. The Association for Computational Linguistics. International Workshop on Computational Linguistics for Uralic Languages 2021, EWPRF 2021 / IWCLUL 2021 ; Conference date: 23-09-2021 Through 25-09-2021.

Susanna Virtanen and Csilla Horváth. 2023. Mansi. In *The Uralic languages, 2nd edition*, pages 665–702, London. Routledge.

Всероссийская Перепись. 2020a. Владение языками и использование языков населением. Part 5, Table 4. Accessed: 2023-04-01.

Всероссийская Перепись. 2020b. Владение языками и использование языков населением. Part 5, Table 17. Accessed: 2023-04-01.

A grammatical analyser for Tokelau

Trond Trosterud
UiT The Arctic University of Norway
trond.trosterud@uit.no

Arnfinn Muruvik Vonen
Oslo Metropolitan University
arnfinn.vonen@oslomet.no

Abstract

This article will present a grammatical analyser, disambiguator and dependency analysis of Tokelau. The grammatical analyser is written as a finite-state transducer (FST), whereas the disambiguator and dependency analyser are written in Constraint Grammar (CG), both within the GiellaLT infrastructure. Contrary to most languages analyzed within this framework, Tokelau is a Polynesian language and thus predominantly isolating language, with reduplication and affixation as the main morphological processes. The discussion on Tokelau will thus also be relevant for an FST and CG treatment of other Polynesian languages.

1 Introduction

This article will present a lexicon, morphological analyser, disambiguator and dependency grammar for Tokelau.

Section 2.1 gives a background of the Tokelau language and the grammatical approach behind the analysis. Section 3 presents the morphological analysis, section 4 discusses disambiguating the Tokelau morphology and analysing it syntactically via a dependency analysis. Section 5 contains an evaluation of the grammatical models, section 6 discusses practical tools derived from the analysers. Finally comes a conclusion.

2 Background

2.1 The Tokelau language

Tokelau, also known in English as Tokelauan, is a Polynesian language, spoken on the Tokelau Islands, a dependent territory of New Zealand located between Samoa and Kiribati in the Pacific Ocean. Being a Polynesian language, Tokelau has a mainly isolating word structure. Affixation is used for such purposes as causativization and nominalization. One interesting category with respect to grammatical analysis is verbal number, which is expressed morphologically on the verb in several ways, particularly reduplication and prefixation, depending partly on the shape of the verbal stem. Verbal number, if present, agrees with the absolutive (bare) noun phrase (see 4.4 below on Tokelau sentence structure). Oblique arguments and adverbials are preposition phrases (Simona, 1986a, p. xxix).

There are comprehensive studies of Tokelau grammar, notably a dissertation on Tokelau noun phrase structure (Vonen, 1997) as well as one on Tokelau syntax in general (Hooper, 1993). The standard dictionary, Simona (1986b), also contains a lengthy grammatical sketch (Simona, 1986a). There are two grammatical handbooks on the language (Hovdhaugen et al., 1989; Hooper, 1996).

The main non-segmental morphological process is syllabic reduplication, where the first syllable of the stem is reduplicated, as shown in Simona (1986a) p. xxvi-xxvii. Example (1) shows the singular and plural forms of two verbs.

(1) a. nofo - nonofo 'sit, live (sg-pl)'
    b. galue - gālulue 'work'

There are also examples of total reduplication, although only on bisyllabic stems. Example (2) shows a shift from neutral to continuative Aktionsart:

(2) a. alo – aloalo
    'paddle – paddle continuously'
    b. logo – logologo
    'tell – tell everyone'

Reduplication has several functions in Tokelau, expressing plural is only one of them. For lexicalised reduplication the best way will be to just

Proceedings of the 9th Workshop on Constraint Grammar and Finite State NLP, pages 38–44
March 5, 2025

list reduplicated forms in the lexicon. Working on the present analyser will help distinguishing between productive and lexicalised reduplication.

Nouns are not inflected. Number is indicated by means of prenominal determiners denoting either singular or plural.

2.2 The grammatical framework behind this study

This study presents a grammatical model of the Tokelau language, using Finite State Transducers and Constraint Grammar, as presented in sections 3 and 4 below. The code itself uses the *GiellaLT* infrastructure (giellalt.github.io). This infrastructure consists of a language-independent set-up of build routines for turning grammatical models into programs analysing running text as well as into practical programs like spellcheckers, grammarcheckers, etc.

A more thorough presentation is given in Moshagen et al. (2023).

2.3 Earlier research on Polynesian language models

To our knowledge, there have not been any attempt so far at building language models for Tokelau[1]. A related work for Māori is Finn et al. (2022b). The main point for the authors is to established a tagset for Māori based upon Māori grammar instead of just copying the tagset from the Universal Dependency framework[2], referred to as a tagset "not fit for non-European languages" (op.cit. p. 6). The same authors also investigate the role the analysis of particles plays in Māori disambiguation, cf. Finn et al. (2022a). Their conclusion is that the part-of-speech (POS) label PARTICLE is glossing over grammatical differences within the class. As a case in point they quote the Māori particle *pai* 'good, well', capable of (pre)modifying both verbs and nouns, thus calling for the terms *adverb* and *adjective*. The authors argue against this, and argue that since *pai* in both cases modifies the word it preceeds, be it nouns or verbs, a POS label MODIFIER (MOD) is a better option. We will return to this issue, arguing for a third solution, in sections 4.1 and 4.3.

Karnes et al. (2023) presents an analysis of Māori based on Universal Dependency. The paper is relevant in this context, since we, too, will present a dependency analysis of Tokelau. Our approach will differ from their UD approach in some respects: In UD, lexical words are mothers of functional words, whereas in our approach functional words act as mothers to lexical words when they govern the distribution of the functional words. Thus, in what phrase structure grammars analyse as PPs, UD sees the preposition as the daughter of the noun, whereas in our (Constraint Grammar) approach the noun is the daughter of the preposition, thus making it possible to distinguish between different verbal arguments. For (phrase structure) PPs, the P is the daughter of the verb, whereas for NPs, the N is the daughter. Within UD, this distinction must be made indirectly, distinguishing between N daughters *without* P daughters (objects etc.) and N daughters *with* P daughters (PPs in phrase structure frameworks). An analysis within our framework may still be converted to UD and vice versa.

3 The Tokelau Finite State Transducer

The Tokelau grammatical model is written as a finite state transducer, as presented in Beesley and Karttunen (2003). The morphophonological rules were written in *twolc*, as first presented in Koskenniemi (1983).

3.1 Morphophonology

With relatively little morphology, the main challenge for the Tokelau morphophonological component is reduplication.

Partial reduplication in finite state transducers was solved by Beesley and Karttunen (2003) (p. 487-493), for twolc. The idea is to use the reduplicating CV sequence as the reference point, and build one rule to copy the C and another to copy the V. In lexc, the reduplication morphology is represented as `^R^E>`, where the > marks the stem boundary and the `^R` and the `^E` the position to copy the C and V, respectively. This is then pointed to the stem lexicon, where we find the reduplicating stems, e.g. *nofo* 'sit'. This string is then applied to the twolc reduplication rules:

```
^R:Cx <=> .#. _ ^E: %> Cx ;
    where Cx in Cns ;

^E:Vx <=> .#. ^R: _ %> (Cns) Vx ;
    where Vx in Vow ;
```

[1]The single exception, less relevant in this context, is Kargaran et al. (2023), which contains language identification models for 1665 languages, one of them for Tokelau.

[2]The authors do not refer to any version of the Universal Dependencies (UD) tagset, but the tagset of UD Version 2 may be found at universaldependencies.org/u/pos/.

In the R:Cx rule, ^R gets it value from the variable Cx (for this stem, n, and in the corresponding rule E:Vx, ^E gets it variable from Vx, here e. The result is the reduplicated form $nonofo$ 'sit (plural)'.

For full reduplication, Beesley and Karttunen (2003) enclosed the string to be reduplicated with two boundary symbols ^[and ^], and then denoted the duplication of the string with an operator, written ^2. An algorithm **compile-replace** would then duplicate the string. For their example language Malay, this would then result in plural forms like $bukubuku$ and $pelabuhanpelabuhan$ from $buku$ 'book' and $pelabuhan$ 'port', respectively.

Now, this algorithm is not available in *hfst-lexc*, the compiler used for the present model of Tokelau. What we instead did, was to utilise the fact that the so-called full reduplication of Tokelau in practice only involves two syllables. We thus extended the analysis above to two syllables. For two-syllable reduplication, we made 4 rules, one for each sound. The two last ones, closest to the stem, were as the ones above, and the two first ones were as follows:

```
^R1:Cx <=> _ ^E1: ^R2: ^E2: %> Cx ;
     where Cx in Cns ;

^E1:Vx <=> _ ^R2: ^E2: %> (Cns) Vx ;
      where Vx in Vow ;
```

Here, each of the four reduplicated letters gets its own value, and the result is *logologo* from ^R1^E1^R2^E2> pointing to *logo*. Note that the same rule will also work for *aloalo*, only with reference to the last three letters.

Since there is only a finite number of verb stems marking plural via reduplication, an alternative option would have been to have two entries in the lexicon, one for the singular form and one for the plural form, both with the singular form as lemma. In our experience, lexicon maintenance is easier with one entry per lemma. A further benefit of modeling the morphological processes explicitly is that it gives a transparent picture of the morphological processes of the language in question, here Tokelau.

3.2 Lexicon and morphology

Tokelau has two open parts of speech, nouns and verbs. For the nouns, we identified a subgroup *location nouns*, the rest were simply given a +N tag.

For the verbs, we modeled number as a morphological process. The reduplication prefixes were added prior to the stem, as shown in section 3.1 above. Some verbs form their plural not with reduplication but with adding a prefix *ta-*, for these we simply added the prefix. Some verbs do not form a distinct plural form, they were marked as ambiguous.

The words belonging to the closed classes were added and provided with tags reflecting their syntactic behaviour.

4 The Tokelau Constraint Grammar

The constraint grammar framework was originally presented in Karlsson (1990). The present implementation is written in *vislcg3*, as presented in Bick (2023).

To put it simply, we distinguished 4 types of particles and based the N/V disambiguation as well as the NP delimitation on four types of functionally defined particles, defined by whether they precede or follow their head word, and by whether the head word is a verb or a noun[3]. Thus, contrary to previous research, we argue for more rather than less types of particles, dependent upon the function they play in the sentence, and in our perspective, dependent upon their ability to delimit noun phrases and verbs.

4.1 Noun phrases

The structure of noun phrases that we are adhering to, is largely in line with the analyses found in Hooper (1996) and Hovdhaugen et al. (1989), although we disagree with them in viewing the preposition not as a part of the noun phrase, but rather as forming a preposition phrase with the NP.

The noun phrase, in our analysis, consists of a determiner (which may, in certain cases, be null), a possible premodifier (typically, a size indicator), a nucleus (a common noun, a proper noun, a locative noun, or a personal pronoun), and possibly one or more postmodifiers (lexical modifiers and/or postmodifying particles) (Example from Simona (1986a, xix).

(3) he | mātuā | ika
this.DET.INDEF:SG | big.PCLE.PRE | fish.N.SG
lele
very.PCLE.POST
'a huge fish'

[3]This is a slight simplification. We also distinguish some specific particles modifying proper nouns or numerals. We will not discuss them here.

The constraint grammar assigns the tag @>N to prenominal determiners and particles and the tag @N< to postnominal demonstratives and particles. Dependency rules then set a dependency relation between the noun and its modifiers, as long as no non-NP constituents (NPNH) occur between the determiner or demonstrative and the noun.

```
MAP (@>N) TARGET Det IF
    (*1 N BARRIER NOT-PRE-N);
MAP (@>N) TARGET Pre IF
    (*1 N BARRIER NOT-PRE-N);
MAP (@N<) TARGET Post IF (*-1 N BARRIER V);
MAP (@N<) TARGET Dem IF (-1 N)(NOT 1 N);

SETPARENT @>N TO (*1 N BARRIER NPNH);
SETPARENT @N< TO (*-1 N BARRIER NPNH);
```

4.2 Preposition phrases

Most noun phrases are complements of prepositions. In the Tokelau constraint grammar, the PP structure is expressed by two rules. First, a MAP rule assigns the syntactic tag @P< ("I am a complement to a **P** to my left") to the N closest to the P. Then, a SETPARENT rule sets a dependency relation between the preposition and the noun complement.

```
MAP (@P<) TARGET N OR Pron IF
    (*-1 Pr BARRIER N OR V);
SETPARENT:r6 @P< TO (*-1 Pr BARRIER V);
```

4.3 The verbal complex

The term *verb phrase* (VP) is usually understood as "the verb and its arguments (except the subject)". Tokelau syntax does not quite work this way, and we will thus avoid the term VP for Tokelau. Instead, we identify the *verbal complex*, by which we mean the main verb, its auxiliaries and verbal particles. Being an isolating language, Tokelau expresses both morphosyntactic categories related to verbs (tense-aspect, negatives) and Aktionsart as verbal particles.

The verbal complex, too, is analysed largely according to Hooper (1993, 52f), but see also Hooper (1996) and Hovdhaugen et al. (1989). The verbal complex consists of a tense-aspect particle (absent in certain functions such as the imperative or the narrative relating of series of events), a possible negative particle, a possible preverbal subject pronoun, a possible prenuclear particle or auxiliary, then the verb. After the verb may follow a postmodifying particle, a possible directional particle, a possible anaphoric particle, and a possible manner particle (Hooper, 1993).

In addition to their occurrence as predicates in verbal sentences, verbs may also occur in nominalized structures, expressed by preposing the singular definite article *te*. In these constructions, tense-aspect particles usually do not occur. The absolutive phrase is replaced with a possessive phrase. These nominalized constructions may be expanded by a nominalizing suffix *-ga*, usually to express past tense. The position of the suffix is usually after the directional particles, and sometimes additionally before the directional particle in (4) (examples, glosses and translations from p. 35 in Hooper (1996):

(4) a. Kāmata loa toku havalivali
begin MAN 1SG.POSS walk.REDUP
mai ki te kakai...
DIR to.PR DET village
'My [habit of] walking to the village began then...'

b. Ko te galo atuga lava tēnā
PR DET disappear DIR-NOM INT DEM
o Lata
of L.
'That was the complete disappearance of Lata.'

The verbal complex is analysed in the same way as the noun phrases discussed in section 4.1.

4.4 Sentence structure

Tokelau is generally considered a verb-initial language. That is, the verbal complex often introduces the sentence, and if a topical or focused noun phrase is preposed to the verbal complex, they are usually marked with the "presentative" preposition *ko*.

The case-marking pattern of the language is ergative: An NP referring to the main argument of an intransitive verb (cf. "non-agentive sentence" in Hovdhaugen et al. (1989) and Hooper (1996)) or the patient of a transitive verb (cf. "agentive sentence" in Hovdhaugen et al. (1989) and Hooper (1996)) is marked as absolutive (i.e., without a preposition), while an NP referring to the agent of a transitive verb is marked as ergative (called "agentive" in Hovdhaugen et al. (1989) and Hooper (1996)) with the preposition *e*. Also verbal number, to the extent that it expresses agreement with the number of an argument of the verb, follows the ergative pattern.

Being an ergative language, Tokelau marks the single argument of an intransitive verb (called **S**)

Test	Words	Coverage
First test	351080	0.9026
3 weeks' development	320540	0.9656

Table 1: Coverage of the New Testament

Test	Words	Coverage
The full text	62281	0.8897
Excl. capitalised words	44442	0.8976

Table 2: Coverage: Min. of Education books

Type	Analyses	An / words
Without disamb	637469	1.66
With disamb	383837	1.17

Table 3: Disambiguating the New Testament

in the same way as the patient argument of a transitive verb (called **P**), whereas the agent argument is marked differently, with the preposition *e* (called **A**). In Constraint Grammar, both the S and the P arguments will be identified as NPS linked to the verb without any intervening preposition for the P also with a PP headed by an *e* preposition to its right or left.

In addition to verbal sentences, the language allows locative, possessive and nominal sentences. Locative and possessive sentences resemble verbal sentences, but they have a locative (*i* 'in, at') or possessive (*a, o*) prepositional phrase in the verbal slot in the verbal complex. Nominal sentences include a presentative prepositional phrase in the verbal slot and usually have no tense-aspect marker or other pre- or post-modifiers characteristic of the verbal complex.

If the NP preceded by the ergative preposition *e* is a personal pronoun, then this referent may alternatively or additionally be expressed by a preverbal pronoun. A preverbal pronoun may also be used if the verb is intransitive, but only if the verbal complex contains the dehortative tense-aspect marker *nahe*.

5 Evaluation

5.1 The FST

The grammatical model was developed by working with the Tokelau grammars and dictionary (Simona, 1986b) and testing it successively against the Tokelau New Testament, including adding names from the New Testament to the grammar model.

The lexicon contained 5780 lemmas during the final test, slightly less during the first one. An important result to notice is that even with a minimal morphology and a very small set of lemmas we were quickly able to achieve a coverage above 95 %.

Testing for text not used for development, we took a totally new genre, the Level 4 books from the Tokelau Ministry of Education (gaganatokelau.org.nz), containing books on a wide range of topics, solar energy, COVID, coral bleaching, ancient navigation, poetry and local governance, to mention a few. The books contained many new names that, contrary to the New Testament, had not been added to the language model. We thus tested the corpus twice for coverage, with and without words having an initial capital letter. Table 1 shows the result for the New Testament and table 2 shows the results for the book corpus. In table 1, "First test" refers to testing the coverage based upon the general lexicon only whereas "3 weeks' development" refers to results after having improved the grammar and (above all) added missing names and words to the lexicon. Needless to say, improving the coverage beyond 96.56 % is certainly doable, the lexicon just needs more work.

Also for table 2, the coverage is quite good, almost 89 % for the full text and almost 90 % when excluding names.

5.2 The constraint grammar

We tested the constraint grammar on the New Testament.

Table 3 shows that each Tokelau word has on average 1.66 different analyses. 21 constraint grammar rules have reduced this number to 1.17, and increasing the number of constraint grammar rules will no doubt bring the disambiguation ratio closer to 1.0.

6 Practical tools

6.1 The spellchecker

The GiellaLT infrastructure offers a ready-made setup for converting transducers into spellcheckers. We did that for Tokelau[4].

A controversial issue in Tokelau orthography is the representation of vowel length, which is

[4]The resulting program may be downloaded via the *Divvun Manager*, available at divvun.no and put to use in Windows, Macintosh and Linux computers.

Test	Words	1st pos	Top 5
NT, long V	315	95.9	98.7

Table 4: Correcting missing length mark

phonemic and may be indicated by a macron above a vowel to indicate that it is long. According to Ministry for Pacific Peoples (2024, p. 7), "support for and against consistent macron use is broadly divided along diaspora and Tokelau lines respectively". Thus, the Government of Tokelau (Matāeke o Akoakoga a Tokelau, n.d.) provides guidelines such as "Don't include macrons where the pronunciation is widely known", while the New Zealand Ministry of Education (Ministry of Education, 2009, p. 14) and Ministry of Pacific Peoples (Ministry for Pacific Peoples, 2024) emphasize the usefulness of macrons for the language learner. In the texts we have worked on so far, there is a tendency to drop the macron whenever a corresponding word with a short vowel does not exist. 55.5 % of the words with long vowel in the Tokelau New Testament recognised by the language model did not have a short vowel counterpart, thus adding vowel length distinguished minimal pairs in 44.5 % of the cases.

In the further development of the spellchecker, we will approach the relevant authorities to make sure that the spellchecker will be in line with the needs of the Tokelau language community. A spellchecker able to correct macron errors (missing or hypercorrect long vowel marks) may easily be changed into a spellchecker tolerating missing macrons or even into one prohibiting macrons.

In order to test the spellchecker's ability to correct missing length marks, we extracted all words containing one long vowel from the New Testament, and removed the length mark. We then made sure that the resulting word was unknown to the language model. This resulted in a t of 315 distinct wordforms. We ran this list through the spellchecker, and measured whether it was able to suggest the correct form as the first correction suggestion or as one of the five corrections in the top five-list (since most spellcheckers offer only 5 suggestions, suggestions further down the list of suggestions were ignored). It turned out that the spellchecker was able to correct length mark omission on 98.7 % of the cases, in 95.9 % of the cases the correction was given in the first position on the suggestion list, cf. table 4.

The cases where the targeted form was not the first suggestion were either forms with more than one potential length error or forms where other suggestions were common words (cf. (5)).

(5) **Halamo → Halāmo, Halamō*
**Ha → Ma, la, Na, Ka, La, Hā*

6.2 The need for a grammarchecker

Since a large part of Tokelau word tokens are short (one and two letters long), we predict the number of real-word errors to be larger than for synthetic languages, having longer words.

Our hypothesis is thus that in an isolating language like Tokelau, a smaller part of text correction is actually linked to orthographic errors, and a larger part to grammatical errors, to what to the proofing tool will look like wrong use of shorter words.

Building a grammarchecker falls outside the scope of the present paper and is left for future research.

7 Conclusion

We have during a short time built a finite state transducer, constraint grammar disambiguator, syntactic function and dependency relation annotator for Tokelau, a Polynesian language spoken on the Tokelau islands and in diaspora communities in New Zealand and elsewhere. The empirical basis for the programs was the standard Tokelau dictionary ((Simona, 1986b)), as well as the standard grammars for the language ((Hooper, 1993, 1996; Vonen, 1997; Hovdhaugen et al., 1989). The result was a language model with relatively high coverage (89 % on unseen text, excluding proper nouns) and relatively high disambiguation rate (1.17 readings/wordform). The resulting transducer has been implemented as a spellchecker for Microsoft Word for Windows and for standard Macintosh programs. Testing shows that it may correct the most common spelling error in Tokelau (vowel length) quite efficiently, 98.7 % of a set of artificially created length errors were corrected, 95.9 % of them as the first suggestion.

Acknowledgments

Thanks to Sjur N. Moshagen for helping out with the implementation of the Tokelau keyboard and proofing tools.

References

Kenneth R. Beesley and Lauri Karttunen. 2003. *Finite State Morphology*. Studies in Computational Linguistics. CSLI Publications, Stanford, California.

Eckhard Bick. 2023. Visl & cg-3: Constraint grammar on the move: An application-driven paradigm. In *Rule-Based Language Technology*, volume 2 of *NEALT Monograph Series*, pages 112–140, University of Tartu. NEALT.

Aoife Finn, Suzanne Duncan, Peter-Lucas Jones, Gianna Leoni, and Keoni Mahelona. 2022a. Annotating "particles" in multiword expressions in te reo Māori for a part-of-speech tagger. In *Proceedings of the 18th Workshop on Multiword Expressions @LREC2022*, pages 67–74, Marseille, France. European Language Resources Association.

Aoife Finn, Peter-Lucas Jones, Keoni Mahelona, Suzanne Duncan, and Gianna Leoni. 2022b. Developing a part-of-speech tagger for te reo Māori. In *Proceedings of the Fifth Workshop on the Use of Computational Methods in the Study of Endangered Languages*, pages 93–98, Dublin, Ireland. Association for Computational Linguistics.

Robin Eliszabeth Hooper. 1996. *Tokelauan*, volume 58 of *Languages of the world Materials*. Lincom Europa, München - Newcastle.

Robin Elizabeth Hooper. 1993. *Studies in Tokelauan syntax*. University of Auckland, Auckland.

Even Hovdhaugen, Ingjerd Hoëm, Consulata Mahina Iosefo, and Arnfinn Muruvik Vonen. 1989. *A handbook of the Tokelau language*. Norwegian University Press and The Institute for Comparative Research in Human Culture, Oslo.

Amir Hossein Kargaran, Ayyoob Imani, François Yvon, and Hinrich Schuetze. 2023. GlotLID: Language identification for low-resource languages. In *Findings of the Association for Computational Linguistics: EMNLP 2023*, pages 6155–6218, Singapore. Association for Computational Linguistics.

Fred Karlsson. 1990. Constraint grammar as a framework for parsing running text. In *COLING '90 Proceedings of the 13th conference on Computational linguistics*, volume 3, pages 168–173, Helsinki.

Sarah Karnes, Rolando Coto, and Sally Akevai Nicholas. 2023. Towards Universal Dependencies in Cook Islands Māori. In *Proceedings of the Sixth Workshop on the Use of Computational Methods in the Study of Endangered Languages*, pages 124–129, Remote. Association for Computational Linguistics.

Kimmo Koskenniemi. 1983. *Two-level Morphology. A General Computational Model for Word-forms Production and Generation*, volume 11 of *Publications of the Department of General Linguistics*. University of Helsinki.

Sjur Nørstebø Moshagen, Flammie Pirinen, Lene Antonsen, Børre Gaup, Inga Mikkelsen, Trond Trosterud, Linda Wiechetek, and Katri Hiovain-Asikainen. 2023. *The GiellaLT infrastructure: A multilingual infrastructure for rule-based NLP*, volume 2 of *NEALT Monograph Series*, pages 70–94. NEALT.

Romati Simona. 1986a. An outline of Tokelau grammar. In *Tokelau Dictionary*, pages xi–xlix. Office of Tokelau Affairs, Western Samoa.

Romati Simona. 1986b. *Tokelau Dictionary*. Office of Tokelau Affairs, Western Samoa.

Arnfinn Muruvik Vonen. 1997. *Parts of speech and lingustic typology. Open classes and conversion in Russian and Tokelau*, volume 22 of *Acta Humaniora*. Det historisk-filosofiske fakultet , University of Oslo.

A Grammar-Based Method for Instilling Empirical Dependency Structure in LLMs

Olle Torstensson and **Oskar Holmström**
Linköping University
{olle.torstensson, oskar.holmstrom}@liu.se

Abstract

We investigate whether synthetic pretraining data generated from a formal grammar modeling syntactic dependencies can improve English language models. Building upon the structured pretraining data approach of Papadimitriou and Jurafsky (2023), we develop a grammar that more closely mirrors empirical dependency structures. Our results are negative – this type of pretraining significantly degrades model performance, with both our and their pretraining approach performing worse than no pretraining at all. We analyze potential explanations for these findings and discuss implications for future work on structured-data pretraining.

1 Introduction

Language learners – human and artificial ones alike – are able to pick up on structural features of natural language without being subjected to any *explicit* structural supervision. Recently, Papadimitriou and Jurafsky (2023) investigated the question of what makes this learning possible – specifically by what *structural biases* it is facilitated (throughout, we will refer to this paper as (PJ23)). In this undertaking, they lean on theories about structural predispositions, such as recursion, being inherent in humans (Hauser et al., 2002). To test this, they instilled an artificial language learner with *structural knowledge* of language, without teaching it anything about the actual *contents* of language. In more practical terms, they pretrained a neural language model on synthetic languages – whose vocabulary consists of integers rather than words – meant to model dependency structures of natural language, in order to then finetune it on actual natural language.

While their main goal was understanding human language acquisition, their results suggest language models may benefit from this pretraining approach. So, with the alternative goal of improving language models, the question of whether there are more suitable pretraining languages for this type of transfer learning arises. We construct a weighted context-free grammar that formally generates one such language, in which the distribution of word dependencies more closely follows that of natural language. The weights in our grammar model the frequencies of dependency links in a given natural language; for higher-resourced languages these frequencies can be directly extracted from dependency treebanks, whereas for lower-resourced languages they would need to be estimated in some other way. Formalisms like Constraint Grammar (Karlsson, 1990) are perfectly capable of this task and well-developed for several low-resourced languages (Pirinen et al., 2023). In such a setting our approach could be particularly valuable since existing linguistic knowledge can be leveraged to increase the speed of model convergence during training without consuming additional textual resources.

We use our generated language to pretrain a neural language model and compare the performance, measured in terms of perplexity after finetuning on English, to that of (PJ23).

2 Background: Word dependencies

Word dependencies appear in both syntactic and semantic analysis of natural language. In the case of syntax, the structure of a sentence is usually represented by a tree (see Figure 1a) in which edges denote dependencies, whereas the semantics may be represented by a directed acyclic graph (DAG) (see Figure 1b). Some subsets of dependencies form recursive patterns, i.e., ones in which edges are nested, whereas others contain crossing edges (see Figure 2). The distribution of dependency lengths (the distance between two dependent words) is largely language-dependent (Oya, 2021)

Proceedings of the 9th Workshop on Constraint Grammar and Finite State NLP, pages 45–49
March 5, 2025

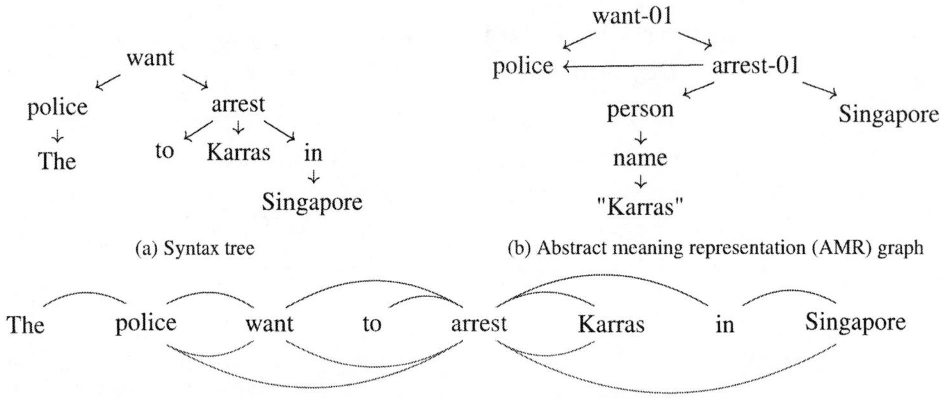

(a) Syntax tree

(b) Abstract meaning representation (AMR) graph

(c) Flattened and undirected version of the syntax tree (top, in blue) and the AMR (bottom, in red)

Figure 1: Syntactic and semantic representations of the sentence *The police want to arrest Karras in Singapore*. Example taken from (Wang et al., 2015).

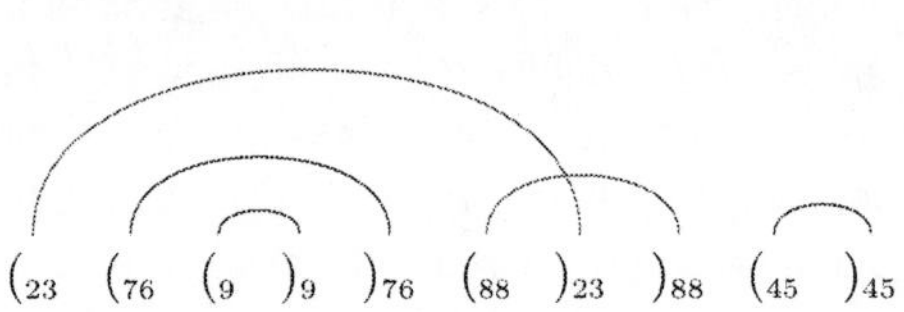

Figure 2: Example string from pretraining data. For the sake of presentation, we view matching numbers as numbered bracket pairs. Crossing edges are marked in red.

and furthermore very much dependent on sentence length (Ferrer-i-Cancho and Liu, 2014).

3 Generating pretraining data

Following (PJ23), to instill knowledge of dependency structure in an untrained neural language model without granting it access to the vocabulary, we generate synthetic pretraining data consisting of numeric sequences (see Figure 2), where matching numbers indicate a dependency between the indices.[1] While our data generation process shares these features with (PJ23), there are some key differences.

3.1 The NEST-MIX-p language of (PJ23)

In (PJ23), the authors define a formal probabilistic model for generating strings which they call NEST-MIX-p, where p is a parameter. A string is constructed sequentially, and at each step a new bracket pair is opened with probability 0.49 and the most recently opened one is closed with probability 0.51 – with the exception that with probability p, a newly opened bracket pair will be a crossing one and its length randomly decided based on an empirical distribution of dependency lengths.[2] This process is continued until the sequence is of length exactly 512.

3.2 Our EMP-DEP language

An advantage of generating the pretraining data in a completely artificial way without relying on an empirical distribution is that one can attempt to model both syntactic and semantic dependencies at the same time. Since we wish to model the dependencies from natural language, a choice between the two is required. Mainly due to data availability, we choose to model our data on *syntactic* dependencies. For the same reason, we also need to commit to a target language from which we model the dependencies already in the pretraining phase (although, technically this is also the case for NEST-MIX-p – see footnote 2).

To synthesize strings, we perform a weighted sampling from a formal language EMP-DEP defined via a *weighted context-free grammar* – a context-free grammar where production rules are equipped with weights, which are then multiplied upon application. In our grammar, these weights represent the frequencies at which a dependency

[1] Thus, dependencies have no direction in these strings.

[2] While the fact that the length of the crossing dependencies follow an empirical distribution makes the language somewhat grounded in reality, the distribution is not exclusive to crossing dependencies and does not take sentence length into account. Note also that because of this, a bias toward a *specific* natural language is introduced.

link between two indices occur in syntactical dependency trees, given the sentence length. Although these frequencies could in principle be estimated with the help of Constraint Grammar or other rule-based methods of dependency parsing, we have opted to utilize the readily available dependency trees found in the English Universal Dependencies Treebank[3]. From this collection of trees, we extract (1) a distribution over sentence lengths; and (2) for each sentence length, a distribution over dependence arcs (i.e., not just their lengths, but also their positions in the sentence).

In what follows, let m be the size of our integer vocabulary, let $n_{\max}$ denote a maximum sentence length, and, for all positive integers n, i, j with $i, j \leq n \leq n_{\max}$, let $p^{(n)}$ denote the (normalized) frequency of sentence length n and let $p_{ij}^{(n)}$ denote the (normalized) frequency of the undirected dependency arc i-j given sentence length n.

Before we define our grammar, we cover a couple of additional notational conventions: for any positive integer k, we let $[k] = \{1, \ldots, k\}$ and $[k]_0 = \{0, \ldots, k\}$, and, for any two non-negative integers i and j, we let $\overline{x}_{[i:j]}$ denote the string $x_i \cdots x_j$. If $i > j$, then $\overline{x}_{[i:j]} = \varepsilon$, where ε denotes the empty string. Finally, we construct EMP-DEP via the weighted context-free grammar $(N, [m-1]_0, P, S)$, defined as follows:

First, let $A = \{u\} \cup \{a_k \mid k \in [m-1]_0\}$, after which we define the set of non-terminals

$$N = \{S\} \cup \{\langle w \rangle \mid w \in A^* \text{ and } |w| \leq n_{\max}\}.$$

Then, for all positive integers $n \leq n_{\max}$ and $k, k_1, \ldots, k_n \in [m-1]_0$, P contains the rules

(1) $S \xrightarrow{p^{(n)}} \langle \underbrace{u \cdots u}_{n} \rangle$

(2) $\langle \overline{x}_{[1:i-1]} \; u \; \overline{x}_{[i+1:j-1]} \; u \; \overline{x}_{[j+1:n]} \rangle \xrightarrow{p_{ij}^{(n)}/m}$
$\langle \overline{x}_{[1:i-1]} \; a_k \; \overline{x}_{[i+1:j-1]} \; a_k \; \overline{x}_{[j+1:n]} \rangle$
for all $i, j \in [n]$ and $x_\ell \in A$, where $\ell \in [n]$, such that $p_{ij}^{(n)} \neq 0$

(3) $\langle \overline{x}_{[1:i-1]} u \overline{x}_{[i+1:n]} \rangle \xrightarrow{1/m} \langle \overline{x}_{[1:i-1]} a_k \overline{x}_{[i+1:n]} \rangle$
for all $i \in [n]$ and $x_\ell \in A$, where $\ell \in [n]$, such that $p_{i\ell}^{(n)} = 0$ or $x_\ell \neq u$

(4) $\langle a_{k_1} \cdots a_{k_n} \rangle \xrightarrow{1} k_1 \cdots k_n$

[3]https://universaldependencies.org/

The elements in A are used to denote whether an index is unassigned (u) or assigned a number k (a_k). Rules (1) produce a non-terminal with a number of unassigned indices depending on the sentence length distribution. Rules (2) pair indices by assigning them the same random number, according to the dependency distribution conditioned on the specific sentence length. Via rules (3), remaining indices that cannot be paired (these will exist, e.g., whenever n is odd) are filled with random numbers. Finally, in rules (4), the strings of numbers themselves are produced.

Generating the pretraining data in this way allows for a virtually unlimited number (depending on parameters) of samples, in which all dependencies appear in empirical data. Note however that dependencies that do not occur *together* empirically in a sentence, may do so in our samples, and that the (non-)crossing property of edges may not be preserved.

4 Experiments

All the necessary code to generate the data and run the experiments can be found at `https://github.com/olletorstensson/emp-dep`.

4.1 Data

For our experiments, we produce two datasets: one generated from our language EMP-DEP, and one generated by the NEST-MIX-0.1 procedure of (PJ23).[4] Following the experimental setup of (PJ23), each dataset consists of 1 billion tokens from a vocabulary of integers in the interval $[0, 499]$, and pretrain a language model each on them. The baseline is a randomly initialized model that is not subjected to any pretraining.[5] We then finetune all three models on the relatively modestly sized WikiText-103 English dataset (Merity et al., 2017) made up of 103 million tokens, and evaluate the models in terms of perplexity on its test set.

4.2 Setup

All three models in the experiments have a 124-million-parameter-sized GPT-2 architecture with a vocabulary size of 50,257 which were (with the exception of the baseline model) trained on the pretraining data for 5,000 steps using a batch size of

[4]While their procedure CROSS performs better than NEST-MIX-0.1 by a small margin, there seems to be no dedicated code or sufficiently precise description of it.

[5]This baseline is different from the one in (PJ23), due to our different end goals (see Section 5).

Pretraining	Perplexity (Mean ± Std)
None (baseline)	36.04 ± 0.07
NEST-MIX-0.1	69.66 ± 6.44
EMP-DEP	261.60 ± 69.29

Table 1: Perplexity of different pretrained models and the baseline on the finetuning test data. Average over 5 random seeds, lower is better.

512. The models are then finetuned on the English data during 2 epochs. To handle the different size of the pretraining and finetuning vocabularies, the new word embeddings are randomly sampled from the old ones as opposed to being randomly initialized, as this has been observed to facilitate transfer learning (Wu et al., 2023).

4.3 Results

The results of the evaluation are given in Table 1. It is clear from these numbers that pretraining in any of the two forms does more harm than good in this experimental setting, and that, in addition, the performance of the model biased using our EMP-DEP language falls far behind the one trained on NEST-MIX-0.1.

5 Discussion

Three key aspects of our results warrant an explanation.

The baseline model performed best. Our experimental setup largely follows that of (PJ23), which in the end might be more adapted to their research question, i.e., *"How is language learning affected by a structural bias?"* than ours, i.e., *"Can language models be improved with a structural bias?"*. Specifically, the effects of pretraining and finetuning data size could play a role here. In their experiments they use a different baseline model from ours, namely an already trained model for which the word embeddings had been resampled (before finetuning), as opposed to a randomly initialized one. It might be the case that the embedding resampling is such a setback that the amount of finetuning data is not enough for such a model to recover from it, whereas our baseline model has no such setback to recover from.

The worst performing model, by far, is ours. In our data generation process, we make a number of compromises. Firstly, the commitment to syntax over semantics results in data that is perhaps less useful for learning some dependencies – especially long-term ones. Secondly, only empirical sentence lengths and dependencies appear in the produced data, without any extrapolation it is probably more difficult for the model to generalize in the finetuning phase. Thirdly, as sentence length is integral to the process, the examples from our data are of variable length, in contrast to the constant length produced by NEST-MIX-0.1. As a consequence, our pretraining language is more difficult for the model to learn[6] and may not model English structure as effectively as NEST-MIX-0.1.

The experiments fail to replicate the results of (PJ23). The fact that the perplexity of our NEST-MIX-0.1-infused model is much higher than reported in (PJ23) has several possible explanations, the most likely of which being that some of the training parameters not presented in (PJ23) differ between the two experiments. Our baseline's superior performance, unlike in (PJ23), results from using different baseline models (see first paragraph).

6 Conclusion and Future Work

In this paper, we have limited ourselves to only investigate the perplexity effects of pretraining a language model on specific structured data. While our results do not demonstrate immediate benefits, it would be valuable to examine whether our model actually learns *anything* useful from our type of pretraining by studying attention patterns. Future research directions include alternative grammars, different model architectures, and more targeted downstream tasks. One promising avenue, suggested by a reviewer, would be hybrid approaches using formalisms like Constraint Grammars to enrich training data with full dependency structure, which could help determine whether adding structural information to lexical information benefits model performance.

As recent work supports the potential of structured pretraining data (Lindemann et al., 2024b; Finn et al., 2017; Krishna et al., 2021; Lindemann et al., 2024a; Wu et al., 2021), the injection of structural biases into language models continues to be an important research direction, particularly for less-resourced languages where synthetic data could compensate for scarce resources.

[6]While the decrease in validation loss during pretraining indicates that the model made progress in this respect, it was higher than for NEST-MIX-0.1 in the end.

Acknowledgements

This work was partially supported by the Wallenberg AI, Autonomous Systems and Software Program (WASP), funded by the Knut and Alice Wallenberg Foundation, and the National Graduate School of Computer Science in Sweden (CUGS). The computations were enabled by the Alvis cluster provided by the National Academic Infrastructure for Supercomputing in Sweden (NAISS), partially funded by the Swedish Research Council through grant agreement no. 2022-06725. We also thank Marco Kuhlmann for inspiring discussions and for providing feedback on an early version of this paper, and Kevin Glocker for assisting with various code-related issues.

References

Ramon Ferrer-i-Cancho and Haitao Liu. 2014. The risks of mixing dependency lengths from sequences of different length. *Glottotheory*, 5(2):143–155.

Chelsea Finn, Pieter Abbeel, and Sergey Levine. 2017. Model-agnostic meta-learning for fast adaptation of deep networks. In *Proceedings of the 34th International Conference on Machine Learning, ICML 2017, Sydney, NSW, Australia, 6-11 August 2017*, volume 70 of *Proceedings of Machine Learning Research*, pages 1126–1135. PMLR.

Marc D. Hauser, Noam Chomsky, and W. Tecumseh Fitch. 2002. The faculty of language: What is it, who has it, and how did it evolve? *Science*, 298(5598):1569–1579.

Fred Karlsson. 1990. Constraint grammar as a framework for parsing running text. In *COLING 1990 Volume 3: Papers presented to the 13th International Conference on Computational Linguistics*.

Kundan Krishna, Jeffrey Bigham, and Zachary C. Lipton. 2021. Does pretraining for summarization require knowledge transfer? In *Findings of the Association for Computational Linguistics: EMNLP 2021*, pages 3178–3189, Punta Cana, Dominican Republic. Association for Computational Linguistics.

Matthias Lindemann, Alexander Koller, and Ivan Titov. 2024a. SIP: Injecting a structural inductive bias into a Seq2Seq model by simulation. In *Proceedings of the 62nd Annual Meeting of the Association for Computational Linguistics (Volume 1: Long Papers)*, pages 6570–6587, Bangkok, Thailand. Association for Computational Linguistics.

Matthias Lindemann, Alexander Koller, and Ivan Titov. 2024b. Strengthening structural inductive biases by pre-training to perform syntactic transformations. In *Proceedings of the 2024 Conference on Empirical Methods in Natural Language Processing*, pages 11558–11573, Miami, Florida, USA. Association for Computational Linguistics.

Stephen Merity, Caiming Xiong, James Bradbury, and Richard Socher. 2017. Pointer sentinel mixture models. In *5th International Conference on Learning Representations, ICLR 2017, Toulon, France, April 24-26, 2017, Conference Track Proceedings*. OpenReview.net.

Masanori Oya. 2021. Three types of average dependency distances of sentences in a multilingual parallel corpus. In *Proceedings of the 35th Pacific Asia Conference on Language, Information and Computation*, pages 652–661, Shanghai, China. Association for Computational Lingustics.

Isabel Papadimitriou and Dan Jurafsky. 2023. Injecting structural hints: Using language models to study inductive biases in language learning. In *Findings of the Association for Computational Linguistics: EMNLP 2023*, pages 8402–8413, Singapore. Association for Computational Linguistics.

Flammie Pirinen, Sjur Moshagen, and Katri Hiovain-Asikainen. 2023. GiellaLT — a stable infrastructure for Nordic minority languages and beyond. In *Proceedings of the 24th Nordic Conference on Computational Linguistics (NoDaLiDa)*, pages 643–649, Tórshavn, Faroe Islands. University of Tartu Library.

Chuan Wang, Nianwen Xue, and Sameer Pradhan. 2015. A transition-based algorithm for AMR parsing. In *Proceedings of the 2015 Conference of the North American Chapter of the Association for Computational Linguistics: Human Language Technologies*, pages 366–375, Denver, Colorado. Association for Computational Linguistics.

Yuhuai Wu, Markus N. Rabe, Wenda Li, Jimmy Ba, Roger B. Grosse, and Christian Szegedy. 2021. LIME: learning inductive bias for primitives of mathematical reasoning. In *Proceedings of the 38th International Conference on Machine Learning, ICML 2021, 18-24 July 2021, Virtual Event*, volume 139 of *Proceedings of Machine Learning Research*, pages 11251–11262. PMLR.

Zhengxuan Wu, Alex Tamkin, and Isabel Papadimitriou. 2023. Oolong: Investigating what makes transfer learning hard with controlled studies. In *Proceedings of the 2023 Conference on Empirical Methods in Natural Language Processing*, pages 3280–3289, Singapore. Association for Computational Linguistics.

Case error corrections for noun phrases containing deverbal attributive nouns in Greenlandic

Judithe Denbæk
Oqaasileriffik / The Language Secretariat of Greenland
judithe@oqaasileriffik.gl

Abstract

This paper presents very early findings using Constraint Grammar (CG) in semantic annotation of a specific type of noun phrases in Greenlandic (Kalaallisut), in which the attributive noun is a nominalized predicative verbal stem. The annotation is used in a grammar checker pipeline for the purpose of making case error correction suggestions.

1 Introduction

The paper presents initial ideas on using semantic valency information in a grammar checker pipeline for Greenlandic, with no significant findings yet. As such, the purpose of this contribution to the workshop *Constraint Grammar and Finite State NLP – Rule-based and hybrid methods and tools for user communities at NoDaLiDa 2025* is mainly an invitation to a fruitful discussion and for the author to gain valuable input from experienced peers. The work is carried out as part of Oqaasileriffik's[1] implementation process of a grammar checker pipeline for Greenlandic. The grammar checker pipeline is developed by Giellatekno[2].

Greenlandic only has 3 major word classes (nouns, verbs and particles) with each their subclasses and lacks adjective as a word class on its own. The formal distinction between the word classes is by their obligatory inflection. Particles have no inflection. Nouns can be inflected in two grammatical cases (*absolutive* (ABS) or *relative*[3] (REL)) and six oblique cases (*ablative* (ABL), *vialis*[4] (VIA), *aeqvalis*[5] (AEQ), *instrumental* (INS), *terminalis*[6] (TRM), *locative* (LOK)). Verbs can be transitive or intransitive and have 4 superordinate moods (*indicative* (IND), *interrogative* (INT), *imperative* (IMP), *optative* (OPT)) and 4 subordinate moods (*causative* (CAU), *conditional* (CON), *contemporative* (CONT), *participial* (PAR)).

The basic word-formation is as follows, where the elements in parentheses are optional and *encl* stands for *enclitic particle*:

```
stem + (suffix(es)) + inflection + (encl)
```

The suffixes have 4 classes: nominalizers, verbalizers, verbal and nominal. The noun class can change several times between the stem and the inflection. Enclitic particles can attach to any word class. Although Greenlandic doesn't have adjectives, adjectival meaning can be translated. There is a class of both genuine nouns, nominal suffixes, and nominalized predicative verbal stems that more frequently function as attributive nouns. These are morphologically or syntactically placed to the right of their stem or head noun. In a simplified glossing style, each type is exemplified below:

adjectival noun

(1) illu qorsuk

illu.SG.ABS qorsuk.SG.ABS
house.SG.ABS green.SG.ABS

'green house'

adjectival nominal suffix

(2) illunnguaq

illu-nnguaq.SG.ABS
house-small.SG.ABS

'small house'

[1] https://oqaasileriffik.gl/
[2] https://giellalt.github.io/proof/gramcheck/GrammarCheckerDocumentation.html
[3] also called *ergative* by some authors
[4] also called *perlative* by some authors
[5] also called *equative* by some authors
[6] also called *allative* by some authors

Proceedings of the 9th Workshop on Constraint Grammar and Finite State NLP, pages 50–58
March 5, 2025 ©2025 University of Tartu Library

nominalized predicative verbal stem as adjectival noun

(3) meeraq nuannaartoq

meeraq.SG.ABS nuannaar-toq.SG.ABS
child.SG.ABS be.happy-PTCP.SG.ABS

'happy child'

For a list of the particular abbreviations used in this paper, the reader is referred to the end of the paper. The interpretation of the diminutive suffix in (2) as being adjectival might not be completely adequate, since the assumption is based on the glossing of it as *'small'* in english and would have been *'lille'* in danish. This example might not have been included if english or danish instead formed the diminutive sense derivationally. Whether the PTCP example in (3) gets interpreted as either adjectival or as relative sentence-like probably depends on the speaker of the language and whether or not the form is lexicalized. Other types of verbal stems can be formed with PTCP, it is not reserved for predicative stems only, and as interesting as it is to explore what types of stems behave more substantival than the predicative stems when PTCP is formed, this subject falls outside the scope of the current paper. The attributive noun, as is shown in example (3), is placed after it's head noun. It is in case and number agreement with the head noun, but in recent years there has been a development in which this structure more or less gets treated in a compound-like manner by speakers of the language, wherein the word order is still the same, but the head noun is inflected in a functionally bare absolutive case and only the attributive noun is inflected in the appropriate case, depending on the function of the noun phrase as a whole. Although this can objectively be viewed as a natural development for the language, until there is consensus among the language users for it's acceptance, for the time being this paper will view them as grammatical errors to be given correction suggestions in a grammar checker.

The development of a grammar checker for Greenlandic is in its infancy, and the infrastructure is developed and made available for adaptations to Greenlandic by Giellatekno[7]. For an introduction to Giellatekno infrastructure, see (Moshagen et al. 2013), and for the description of Giellatekno's grammar checker module, see (Wiechetek et. al. 2019).

[7]`https://giellalt.github.io/proof/gramcheck/GrammarCheckerDocumentation.html`

2 Predicative verbal stems

The verbal stems that are termed predicative verbal stems in this paper are semantically portmanteau. They contain both a copular verbal element and an adjectival meaning. This combination of meanings is borne by a single stem that may or may not be comprised of more than one morpheme that in turn might or might not be lexicalized (this subject needs it's own investigation). In their verbal form, provided that the stem is not transitivized, they predicate the subject of the sentence. Take a look at the example (3) from the previous section without the PTCP and with indicative inflection:

(4) meeraq nuannaarpoq

meeraq.SG.ABS nuannaar-IND-3SG
child.SG.ABS be.happy-IND.3SG

'the child is happy'

One would think that an extension of the morphology (i.e. the PTCP form) of a word would add to its semantics, but in this case at least cross-linguistically speaking there seems to be a reduction, perhaps as would be expected with a nominal participle that semantically denotes a resulting state of the stem to which it is attached. The copular element seems to be wiped out and we are left with the semantics of the adjectival part. The copular element can resurface by word formation, for instance, when there is added adverbial-like suffix(es), such as negation, between the predicative stem and the PTCP. In such cases, the PTCP often corresponds to relative sentences in other languages:

(5) meeraq nuannaanngitsoq

meeraq.SG.ABS nuannaa-nngit-soq.SG.ABS
child.SG.ABS be.happy-NEG-PTCP.SG.ABS

'a child who is not happy'

3 Semantic classification for Greenlandic

The semantic classification used in Oqaasileriffik's semantically annotated lexical database, Katersat[8], is based on, or rather, inspired by the system developed in The Danish FrameNet project[9], developed by the University of Southern Denmark and GrammarSoft Aps[10].

[8]`https://oqaasileriffik.gl/en/dict/`
[9]`https://FrameNet.dk`
[10]`https://grammarsoft.com/`

For the predicative verb stems in Greenlandic, the general semantic frame is called "be_attribute, Be" which in some cases has been combined with an additional secondary semantic tag for adjectives. The semantic tags for adjectives are in square brackets starting with a "j". The tag for the word *happy* would be <jpsych>, which is defined as *"psychological, feeling, intellectual, inherent character trait"* and is attributed to nouns that are semantically classified as human, acts and semantics: <H>, <act> and <sem> (Bick, 2019).

In this paper, a combination of verbal frame and prototypes for adjectives will be used in tagging predicative verbal stems. The use of adjectival prototype tags is in purely semantic sense, since the adjectival words in question actually belong to nouns. In PTCP word-formations, this combination of verbal frame and adjectival semantic prototype will be split in purely adjectival prototype and verbal stem frame. By keeping the verbal stem frame tag, the *"pertainym"*[11] relation is informed.

4 Semantic annotation for predicative verbal stems in Greenlandic

Giellatekno grammar checkers already use semantic valency information in their grammar checker pipelines (Wiechetek, 2017). Oqaasileriffik has a semantic module for Oqaasileriffik's analyzer that combines FST[12] analysis with the semantically annotated lexical database, the aforementioned Katersat. This module is not implemented or implementable in the grammar checker for Greenlandic as of December 2024. For this reason for the purpose of this presentation, the annotations are done manually in a CG file within the pipeline for the grammar checker. Example (3) and (4) are annotated in this manner, with output as shown in CG-3 IDE[13]:

input string: (3) meeraq nuannaartoq
CG-3 IDE output:

```
"<meeraq>"
    "meeraq" N Abs Sg <H> §TH
    ADD:68 ADD:92
"<nuannaartoq>"
    "nuannaar" Gram/IV TUQ Der/vn N
    Abs Sg <STEM:f:be_attribute_jpsych>
    <jpsych> <p:<H>_N_Prop>
    ADD:72 ADD:85 SUBSTITUTE:95
    SUBSTITUTE:96
    "nuannaar" Gram/IV V Par 3Sg
    <f:be_attribute_jpsych>
    <§TH_@SUBJ_<H>_N_Abs>
    ADD:72 ADD:85
```

input string: (4) meeraq nuannaarpoq
CG-3 IDE output:

```
"<meeraq>"
    "meeraq" N Abs Sg <H> §TH
    ADD:68 ADD:92
"<nuannaarpoq>"
    "nuannaar" Gram/IV V Ind 3Sg
    <f:be_attribute_jpsych>
    <§TH_@SUBJ_<H>_N_Abs>
    ADD:72 ADD:85
```

Grammarsoft Aps uses <fn:..> as tags for semantic frames, where *"fn"* probably stands for FrameNet. The examples in this paper are just <f:..>, where *"f"* stands for frame.

The CG rules in question are as follows.

definitions:

```
LIST human = "meeraq" ;
LIST objectmarking =
(/[1-4][SP][gl]O/r) ;
LIST subjectmarking =
(/[1-4][SP][gl]/r) ;
SET ITR_pers = subjectmarking
- objectmarking ;
LIST frame = /<f:.*>/r ;
LIST jsem = /<j.*>/r ;
LIST noun_number = (N Sg) (N Pl) ;
LIST-TAGS +=
<f:be_attribute_jpsych>
<H>
<jpsych>
<§TH_@SUBJ_<H>_N_Abs>
<p:<H>_N_Prop> ;
LIST be_attribute_jpsych =
"ajuallap" "pilluar" "nuannaar"
"uumila" ;
```

Both "objectmarking" and "subjectmarking" are defined in order for the rules to specify an intransitive verb ITR_pers. Transitive verbs are easier to capture in rules by simply saying any person (1-4) in any number (Sg or Pl) with the letter for object O at the end, whereas capturing a verbal form by it's subject inflection will work on both transitive and intransitive inflection, so an intransitive verb is defined as subject marking and no object marking. In order to be able to control where the semantic tags go in the cohort, both "any frame tag" and "any adjective prototype tag" are defined within regular expressions. Regular expressions are formulated in slashes ending in the letter "r"[14], /<f:.*>/r means any tag (square brackets) for semantic frames (starts with an f followed

[11] https://aclanthology.org/W19-0406.pdf
[12] Finite State Transducer
[13] https://edu.visl.dk/cg3.html
[14] https://edu.visl.dk/cg3/chunked/tags.html#regex-icase

by a colon) followed by any number of any character ".*". The LIST-TAGS += enables definition of multiple tags.

annotations for input: "nuannaarpoq" in
(4) meeraq nuannaarpoq

```
ADD:73 <f:be_attribute_jpsych>
AFTER ITR_pers OR noun_number
be_attribute_jpsych ;
ADD:85 <§TH_@SUBJ_<H>_N_Abs>
AFTER frame <f:be_attribute_jpsych> ;
```

Whether or not to include keywords such as TARGET and IF is a question of personal taste or idea of readability. The formal expression of the ADD rule can be read in the Constraint Grammar Manual[15] (Didriksen, 2010). In the example above (ADD:73), the keyword TARGET would have been right before be_attribute_jpsych, which is the definition for different stems, including the stem "nuannaar" in example (4). The predicative verb in the example is intransitive, and the rule adds the tag <f:be_attribute_jpsych> after the person and number inflection, whether it is a predicative verb or a nominalized predicative verbal stem expressing a psychological state (be_attribute_jpsych). The rule ADD:85 is an attempt at defining the frame template for the frame that is added at ADD:73, and the tag is placed after the frame tag. The frame template is a formulation of dependency slots. We expect that the syntactic function of the subject @SUBJ has the semantic role §TH[16] (theme), and that it is of a semantic prototype human <H>, which is a noun in absolutive case <§TH_@SUBJ_<H>_N_Abs>.

tagging for input: "meeraq" in
(4) meeraq nuannaarpoq

```
ADD:69 <H> human | Pron
+ (/[12][SP][gl]/r) ;
ADD:90 §TH <H> + Abs
+ (/\([SP][gl]\)/r)
(*1 <f:be_attribute_jpsych>
+ <§TH_@SUBJ_<H>_N_Abs>
LINK 0 (VSTR:/^[1-4]$1$/r)
- objectmarking) ;
```

The rule ADD:69 adds the tag <H> to the list called "human", where the noun "meeraq" is defined. The rule ADD:90 adds the semantic role tag §TH to the noun that is tagged as human <H>, which is in absolutive case. The absolutive case is the case that is used for the subject of an intransitive verb. The number is formulated as being in agreement with the (person and) number that the verb of the sentence is inflected for. The agreement is expressed in a variable string[17]. The absolutive can be singular or plural:

```
(/\([SP][gl]\)/r)
```

the regular expression group match is in escaped parentheses, and is matched with the variable string match $1 in:

```
(VSTR:/^[1-4]$1$/r)
```

One could consider adding the semantic role tag @SC (subject predicative/complement)[18], in case the tag is to be used cross-linguistically, e.g. for MT[19] purposes.

tagging for input: "nuannaartoq" in
(3) meeraq nuannaartoq

```
SUBSTITUTE:95 (/<f:.*_j.*>/r)
(<STEM:$1$2>v <$2>v) TARGET
(<\(f:be_attribute_\)\(j.*\)>r)
+ TUQ + noun_number ;
SUBSTITUTE:96 <§TH_@SUBJ_<H>_N_Abs>
<p:<H>_N_Prop> AFTER jsem <jpsych> ;
```

The rule SUBSTITUTE:95 splits the tag in two, where <f:be_attribute_jpsych> is split in <STEM:f:be_attribute_jpsych> and <jpsych>, when the predicative verbal stem is in PTCP form. SUBSTITUTE:96 changes the frame template with specification of head type, which in this case is a human prototype noun or proper noun.

5 Quantitive predicative stem with an intensifier

The following example will be of another type of predicative verbal stem, namely <jquant> *"quantitive"* that combines with countable head nouns. Countable nouns are in this paper tagged with <+countable>[20]. This combination of <jquant> and <+countable> will be used to demonstrate case error correction.

In this noun phrase type, there is a free adverbial particle between the head noun and the attributive noun. This structure is chosen for the case correction, because the context provides us with means to find potential errors within Oqaasileriffik's corpus[21] more easily than if we were to

[15]https://edu.visl.dk/cg3/chunked/rules.html#add

[16]https://edu.visl.dk/tagset_cg_all.pdf

[17]https://edu.visl.dk/cg3/chunked/tags.html#variable-strings

[18]https://edu.visl.dk/tagset_cg_all.pdf

[19]Machine Translation

[20]square brackets might have been preferable as feature tags for the sake of distinction from semantic tags

[21]https://oqaasileriffik.gl/en/langtech/corpus/

search for two adjacent nouns where the first is in absolutive case and the next one is in another form of case. The adverbial particle between the head noun and the attributive noun is *taama* (*"so"*, *"as"*, *"that"*), and it is in this structure inseparable with the deverbal suffix -tigə- that is suffixed between the predicative verbal stem and the PTCP:

(6) *ukiut taama amerlatigisuni inuusuttunik atuartitsisarsimavoq

ukioq.PL.ABS taama
year.PL.ABS that
amerla-tigi-su.PL.LOK
be.many-that-PTCP.PL.LOK
inuusuttoq-PL.INS
young.people-PL.INS
atuartit-si-sar-sima-IND-3SG
teach-HTR-HAB-PST-IND-3SG

'(he/she) has been teaching young people for that many years'

When the predicative verbal stem has an adjectival sense, the combination of *taama* and -tigə- is in equative sense (i.e. *as beautiful as*, *as clever as*). In example (6) above, when the predicative verbal stem in question (*amerla-*) is in quantitive sense (be.many), the combination of the adverbial *taama* and the suffix -tigə- instead functions as an intensifier (i.e. *that many*).

The word in need of case error correction in example (6) is *ukiut*, which is in absolutive case. The case needs to be corrected to locative, *ukiuni*, since the noun phrase is meant to be an adverbial phrase in locative case, as indicated by the case of the attributive noun.

The correction is handled in the grammar checker file:

```
WITH Abs + <+countable> + $$NUMERUS
(1 ("taama") LINK 1 TIGE + <jquant> +
$$NUMERUS)
{
ADD:msyn-abs-taama-case
&msyn-abs-taama-case (*) ;

COPY:msyn-abs-taama-case
(VSTR:$1 &SUGGEST) EXCEPT
(Abs &msyn-abs-taama-case)
BEFORE NUMERUS (*)
(2 (/^\(Rel|Abl|Via|Aeq|Ins
|Trm|Lok\)$/r)) ;

ADDRELATION:msyn-abs-taama-case
($2 RIGHT) (*) TO (jC1 (*)) ;
} ;
```

The rules are grouped with the WITH rule (see Swanson et al., 2023). We want to capture what is on the same line as the keyword WITH, which is a countable noun in absolutive case, and which is in the same number $$NUMERUS as another word which is defined in the context. The context is defined on the next line in parenthesis. The word immediately to the right of the head in absolutive case is "taama", and the second word to the right contains the suffix TIGE, has the adjectival semantic prototype tag <jquant> and has the same number inflection as the head in absolutive case. The 3 rules within the curly brackets apply to the context that is defined before the curly brackets. The ADD rule adds a grammar checker tag starting with an ampersand, &msyn-abs-taama-case, the asterisk in the parenthesis refers to the noun in absolutive case that is specified in the same line as the operator WITH. The COPY rule duplicates the reading with the &msyn-abs-taama-case tag, replacing this tag with another tag &SUGGEST that is used in the grammar checker pipeline to suggest corrections. Furthermore the duplicated reading replaces the absolutive case with whatever the case that the attributive noun in PTCP is in, formulated with a variable string.

The suggestion output in the grammar checker is as follows:

error:
ukiut taama amerlatigisuni
correction:
ukiuni taama amerlatigisuni

The feedbacks provided to the user are as replicated below:

```
There should be case (and number)
agreement in noun phrases

The case ending of "ukiut"
needs to be the same as
the case ending of "amerlatigisuni"
```

Specifying combinatorial requirements for a lexical element according to it's semantic features in this manner is practical in determining whether or not for example the noun in absolutive case in question actually is correct, by additionally defining semantic restrictions on the verb of the sentence. The frame for the verb in the example in question is "teach", and the form is in intransitive. The transitive form of the verbal stem that denotes "teach" is detransitivized with the so-called half-transitive[22] suffix, which means that the syntactic subject of the verb with the semantic role of agent

[22] also called antipassive by some authors

is in absolutive case, and what would have been the object of the transitive form is in instrumental case (oblique object in instrumental case). In our particular example, the disambiguation is straightforward in that there has to be person and number agreement between subject and inflection for subject in the verb. The noun in question in our example *ukiut* is in plural, whereas the verb is inflected for a subject in singular. Greenlandic is a pro-drop language, and the subject in the example is implicit. If however the inflection for the subject in the verb had been in plural, morphological information alone would not be sufficient to determine if the noun is semantically compatible as the subject of the sentence, and we would have to rely on ad hoc list definition for what the particular verbal stem could have as a subject.

Our rules need an addition to their contextual requirements in the file containing semantic annotation rules:

```
LIST hum_hum =
(/"atuar"\ Gram/.V\ TIP\ Der/vv\ Gram/../1)
<f:teach> ;
SET nonhum = (<.*>r) - (<H.+>r) ;
ADD <f:teach> AFTER objectmarking
OR ITR_pers hum_hum ;
ADD
<$AG_@SUBJ_<H>_N_Rel-§BEN_@OBJ_<H>_N_Abs>
AFTER frame <f:teach> + objectmarking ;
ADD
<$AG_@SUBJ_<H>_N_Abs-§BEN_@OBJ_<H>_N_Ins>
AFTER frame <f:teach> + ITR_pers ;
```

in the grammar checker file we add:

```
(NEGATE 0 <H> + (VSTR:$1)
LINK *1 V + hum_hum
+ ITR_pers +
(/^[34]\([SP][gl]\)$/r))
```

In short, the verb of the sentence (teach) is a human to human verb (both subject and object are human). We don't wan't to make corrections in cases where the absolutive human noun might be in number agreement with the subject inflection of the intransitive verb, because the noun in absolutive case then could be the subject of the sentence.

6 Exceptions

Oqaasileriffik's corpus has a total of 1.443 sentences that contains the phrasetype

```
Abs + taama
+ [predicative_verb_stem+TIGE+PTCP
+non-absolutive case]
```

A quick glance at these examples shows plenty of instances where the first part in the absolutive case needs no correction. In those instances, there is in most cases a clear violation of semantic combinatorial restrictions between the head noun and the attributive noun, indicating that the noun in absolutive is not to be corrected, but perhaps more likely is the subject of an intransitive subordinate or superordinate verb in the sentence. The examples below start with the Greenlandic sentence, where the noun phrase in focus is in boldface and translated to English below the sentence. The incompatibility between the semantic prototype of the head noun before the particle *taama* and the attributive noun after *taama* are shown below in English, and the translation of the whole phrases is also provided. Case is indicated in square brackets. These square brackets in the following examples have no function and are not used as feature tags:

(7) Taamaattumik **Inughuit taama sakkortutigisumik** isummersinnaasoqalersimappata tamanna tupigineqassanngilluinnarpoq

Inughuit that harsh(ly)

"Therefore it absolutely shouldn't be a surprise to anyone if someone among the **Inughuit** *has acquired the ability to express their opinions* **that harshly**"

```
<H> [ABS] "taama" <jdegree> [INS]
```

(8) Niaqorornaveeqqutitik qallersaassuatillu peeriarlugit tamanut tamaanga igiinnarsimavaat, **kinaluunniimmi taama kiatsigisumi** meqqulualissuarmik qallersaateqarluni sininnavianngimmat.

nobody (in) that warm

"They had removed their helmets and their thick outerwear and spread them all over the place, **nobody** *could sleep* **in (a place) that warm** *wearing outerwear with down (in it)"*

```
<H> [Abs] "taama" <jtemp> [LOK]
```

this particular word-form to denote "warm" is not compatible for metaphoric or literal use to describe humans in Greenlandic. This ambiguity can be resolved with a domain tag for weather specific adjectives <Dweather>[23]

[23]https://edu.visl.dk/semantic_prototypes_adj.pdf

(9) Taamani sikorsuaqarnera pillugu **umiarsuit taama sivisutigisumik** uninngapput Nuup umiarsualiviani.

ships that long

"Back then, the **ships** *were docked in the harbor for* **that long**, *because of storis (a floating mass of closely crowded icebergs and floes*[24]*)"*

`<Vwater> [Abs] "taama" <jtime> [INS]`

this particular word-form to denote "long" is for temporal use only in Greenlandic

(10) **Apeqqutissaralu taama inuusutsigisumut** angivallaassagaluarnersoq neriuppunga silassorissunnguugavit akisinnaassagit

and my question (to) that young

*"***And** *I hope that since you are so clever, that you can tell whether or not my* **question** *would be too big* **for such a young (person)***"*

`<sem-s> [Abs] + taama + <jage> [TRM]`

(11) niaqqi qattornup qulaagut nuisippaa, **kinguninngualu taama sukkatigisumik** tarrisillugu

right after that quick(ly)

"he/she/it let his/her/its head appear at the top of the hill, and made it disappear **as quickly** *(as it had appeared)* **right afterwards***"*

`<temp> [Abs] + taama + <jspeed> [INS]`

(12) piginnittuanulli **kusaginninnini taama sukkatigisumik** takutippaa

her/his admiration that quick(ly)

"but he/she showed **his/her admiration** *to the owner* **that quickly***"*

`<f-psych> [Abs] + taama + <jspeed> [INS]`

(13) **pajugutaali taama sukkatigisumik** utertinneqarpoq

his/her gift that quick(ly)

"but **his/her gift** *was returned* **that quickly***"*

`<cc> [Abs] + taama + <jspeed> [INS]`

The instrumental case is used for 3 main functions in Greenlandic: oblique object (when the main verb is halftransitive[25]), modifier to an incorporated[26] object, or manner adverbial. The latter category is interesting in our examples, since all the instrumental cases that are used in the examples are used adverbially. These examples are perhaps comparable to danish so-called t-adverbials, that are formed by adding a -t on adjectives [27], and are categorized in 3 different types: *manner*, *time* and *degree*. Notice that this is consistent with our examples: (7) <jdegree> (9) <jtime>, and (11) + (12) + (13) falls into the broader category *manner*, namely <jspeed>.

At the moment, Oqaasileriffik's corpus is not available in semantically annotated version. The next step in this pilot project would be to extract those total of 1.443 sentences from corpus and have them parsed with their semantic annotations, manually identify case errors in the head noun, formulate further semantically compatibility restrictions, and make case error corrections in the grammar checker that later can be used for accuracy testing purposes.

7 Concluding remarks

The pilot project described in this paper is unfortunately at its very early beginning and, for this reason, the paper has not been able to show any statistics for accuracy testing. What the findings show is that there is a crucial need to define semantic compatibility restrictions where morphological information does not suffice. This would prevent false positives. Furthermore, the frame information used for predicative verbs needs to be made more specific by adding information about the prototype for the attributive meaning that the nominalized version in PTCP would have, in order to use them to describe their combinatorial restrictions in an accurate manner.

[24] *https://www.merriam-webster.com/dictionary/storis?fbclid=IwZXh0bgNhZW0CMTEAAR3zaIs8MNtCW4Ja-D8viUx-_tIZLNSUs6ENW5JKyL-2sh71vf1KZXZv2i0_aem_AYFjJKn7WSz_3CP1QLnqig*

[25] also called *antipassive* by some authors

[26] also called *inderived* by some authors

[27] https://sproget.dk/typiske-problemer/adverbielt-t-biords-t/

8 List of abbreviations, semantic prototype labels and semantic frames

ABL	ablative case
ABS	absolutive case
AEQ	aequalis case[28]
CAU	causative mood
CON	conditional mood
CONT	contemporative mood
HAB	habitual aspect
HTR	halftransitive suffix
IMP	imperative mood
IND	indicative mood
INS	instrumental case
INT	interrogative mood
LOK	locative case
NEG	negation
OPT	optative mood
PAR	participial mood
PL	plural
PST	past[29]
PTCP	nominal participle[30]
REL	relative case
SG	singular
TRM	terminalis case[31]
VIA	vialis case[32]
3SG	third person singular
`<cc>`	object countable
`<+countable>`	countable noun
`<f-psych>`	feature psychological
`<H>`	human
`<jage>`	age
`<jdegree>`	degree, intensity
`<jspeed>`	speed
`<jtemp>`	temperature
`<jtime>`	time
`<sem-s>`	semiotic, speech
`<temp>`	temporal
`<Vwater>`	vehicle water

[28] also called *equative* by some authors

[29] In the form of a suffix. Tense is not a grammatical category in Greenlandic.

[30] also called *active participle* by some authors

[31] also called *terminative* or *allative* by some authors

[32] also called *perlative* by some authors

Acknowledgements

I would like to extend my gratitude to the welcome reception I have been given, when visiting Giellatekno during late 2023 and 2024, Trond Trosterud (Professor of Sámi computational linguistics, leader of the research group Giellatekno. Department of Language and Culture) who first introduced me to Giellatekno's grammar checker (among many other things), Linda Wiechetek (Senioringeniør. Department of Language and Culture) who spent a great deal of her time to give me a thorough introduction, Kevin Brubeck Unhammer (Trigram AS) for taking time in giving a helping hand with grammar checker CG-related issues whenever needed, Sjur Nørstebø Moshagen (Sjefsingeniør / leiar for Divvun-gruppa Institutt for språk og kultur) and Flammie Pirinen (Engineer. Department of Language and Culture) for technical support whenever needed, last but not least Tino Didriksen who not only tirelessly answers any CG-related questions that I have, but also has been assisting in the whole process of implementing the grammar checker pipeline to Greenlandic.

9 Bibliography

Daniel Swanson, Tino Didriksen, and Francis M. Tyers. 2023. WITH Context: Adding Rule-Grouping to VISL CG-3. In Proceedings of the NoDaLiDa 2023 Workshop on Constraint Grammar - Methods, Tools and Applications, pages 10–14, Tórshavn, Faroe Islands. Association of Computational Linguistics.

Eckhard Bick. 2019. A Semantic Ontology of Danish Adjectives. IN: Simon Dobnik, Stergios Chatzikyriakidis, Vera Demberg, (eds.), *Proceedings of the 13th International Conference on Computational Semantics – Long Papers*. May 2019. Gothenburg, Sweden. Association for Computational Linguistics. pp. 71-78. https://aclanthology.org/W19-0406/

Kenneth R. Beesley, Lauri Karttunen. 2003. Finite State Morphology. CSLI Studies in Computational Linguistics. CSLI Publications. Linda Wiechetek. 2017. "When grammar can't be trusted – Valency and semantic categories in North Sámi syntactic analysis and error detection". A dissertation for the degree of Philosophiae Doctor. Department of Language and Culture (ISK). December 2017.

Linda Wiechetek, Sjur Nørstebø Moshagen, Børre Gaup, and Thomas Omma. 2019. Many shades of grammar checking – launching a constraint grammar tool for North Sámi. IN: *Proceedings of the NoDaLiDa 2019 Workshop on Constraint Grammar - Methods, Tools and Applications*, NEALT Proceedings Series 33:8, pages 35–44.

Sjur N. Moshagen, Tommi A. Pirinen, and Trond Trosterud. 2013. Building an open-source development infrastructure for language technology projects. IN: NODALIDA.

Tino Didriksen. 2010. Constraint Grammar Manual. 3rd version of the CG formalism variant. GrammarSoft ApS, Denmark. http://visl.sdu.dk/cg3/vislcg3.pdf

Divvunspell—Finite-State Spell-Checking and Correction on Modern Platforms

Flammie A Pirinen
Divvun
UiT—Norgga árktalaš universitehta
Tromsø, Norway
flammie.pirinen@uit.no

Sjur Nørstebø Moshagen
Divvun
UiT—Norgga árktalaš universitehta
Tromsø, Norway
sjur.n.moshagen@uit.no

Abstract

Spell-checking and correction is one of the key applications of natural language support. Historically, for the biggest, less morphologically complex languages, spell-checking and correction could be implemented by relatively simple means; however, for morphologically complex and low-resource languages, the solutions were often suboptimal. Finite-state methods are the state of the art in rule-based natural language processing and also for spell-checking and correction they have been effectively used. In this article, we show some recent developments of a finite-state spell-checker implementation that works with modern operating systems and platforms.

1 Introduction

Spell-checking and correction is one of the most basic and most important applications of natural language processing for standardised, written languages. A spell-checker works as a tool for all of the writers of the language, ensuring that most of the texts written follow a norm that is enforced by the tool. This has enormous significance for the text production in the language, which in turn is becoming more and more important in the era of large language models. A large language model is built on huge quantities of texts written by humans, and an underlying expectation is that the majority of the text is written in a standard, norm-abiding language form.

Traditionally spell-checkers have been readily available for morphologically simple languages but have had more limited success for more morphologically complex languages; for example, to this day hunspell is popularly used for a lot of platforms on a computer as a default spell-checker engine. Hunspell itself being developed because previous systems were insufficient for Hungarian morphology, it moreover is limited for other morphologically complex languages. Another approach to spell-checking that is popular in contemporary systems is data-based, either statistical or neural network, this is what many of the autocorrect and autocomplete style models are based on. This, on the other hand, limits the low-resourced languages out of the equation.

The main contribution of this article is recent developments in our implementation of *finite-state spell-checking*, as well as relevant tooling and automation. Finite-state spell-checking works for morphologically complex languages and does not necessarily require any training data, making it suitable for low-resource use cases. One emphasis of this article is the developments related to full end-user use case of the method that the software is not merely an academic experiment but a product that can be installed and used by the language users. For this purpose, we have developed automated evaluation methodology as well as systems for automatically distributing the new changes to end-users.

Following the recent trends of the language technology, that is the break-throughs of the large language models and neural networks, we evaluate our system and compare it to an out of the box neural network in a basic spell-checking and correction task. While the evaluation we perform here is quite rudimentary as a neural network application, it builds towards the research question of: how and to which extents and in which parts of a spell-checking and correcting system shall the large language models be used in hybrid with existing finite-state and rule-based solutions.

2 Background

Spell-checking and correction is an application of natural language processing that has been stud-

Proceedings of the 9th Workshop on Constraint Grammar and Finite State NLP, pages 59–63
March 5, 2025 ©2025 University of Tartu Library

ied since the 1950's. The earliest models worked in practice based on static lists of correctly written word-forms to check against, then slowly adding support for morphological processes as larger vocabularies and more morphologically complex languages were implemented. The most widely spread versions of the spell-checkers used in personal computers are commonly known as `*spell` software, from original SPELL to ispell, aspell, myspell, hunspell and nuspell. Still, these have been difficult to adapt for morphologically rich languages, so for specific languages softwares like zemberek for Turkish and hspell for Hebrew have been developed

Parallel to dictionary-based spell-checkers there has been statistical approaches to spell-checking. This is based on learning a language model from large correctly written texts, one of the most influential models here is (Norvig, 2010). This line of models is usually a basis in most of the mobile auto-complete and autocorrect style systems, nowadays likely based on generative neural network models.

The most basic tool for modeling errors is based on the invention of edit distance, where the errors are modeled as a combination of missing a letter, adding an extra letter, using a wrong letter, or swapping two adjacent letters, first introduced by Levenshtein (1966). Other common ideas that have been used include listing common confusables altogether, trying to map phonemic errors to the writing system various ways, and weighing the mistakes made on a keyboard by the keyboard layout.

One of the most popular ways of handling word-forms of morphologically complex languages is Finite State Morphology (Beesley and Karttunen, 2003), this is often considered the state of the art in handling rule-based language modeling of morphologically context low-resourced languages to this date. The finite-state formulation of spell checking with statistically trained language and error models has been researched by Pirinen et al. (2014). This type of models is also used by the spell-checking and correction solution we are presenting in this article.

3 Methods

Finite-state spell-checking is based on using finite-state automata to model both the correctly spelled words (language model) and mapping of the misspellings from incorrect forms to correct word-forms. In finite-state format this means that there is an automaton that accepts the correctly spelled word-forms and does not accept incorrectly spelled word-forms, and another two-tape automaton that can relate incorrectly spelled word-forms to correctly spelled word-forms. The automata can be weighted and thus give an ordering to correction suggestions as well as likelihoods for the words of the languages in general. This model has been introduced by at least Pirinen and Lindén (2010), and the software introduced here is based on the same finite-state formulation. For language models we have used freely available open source finite-state models from the GiellaLT infrastructure (Pirinen et al., 2023).

The *divvunspell*[1] software we introduce in this article is implemented in the Rust programming language and has bindings and implementations for modern operating systems and mobile platforms: macOS systemwide, Windows systemwide and in MS Office, LibreOffice on all desktop systems, and in iOS and Android keyboard apps. There is also a REST API for web-based clients[2]. We have implemented some basic improvements to the engineering and efficiency as well as correctness of the software. The published version is both light-weight and fast enough to be used as an interactive spelling checker on average end-users' mobile platforms. We have fine-tuned the error-correction algorithm with adjustable weights in the errors made in word-initial, word-medial and word-final positions separately; in the the current version a spelling error in the first or last letter of the word adds triple the weight of an error in the mid-word unless configured otherwise.[3] We have also developed an automated evaluation software for the spell-checking software that can ensure the quality of the spell-checking models does not degrade, as well as a continuous integration and deployment system that can distribute the models to the end users when the dictionaries or grammars of language models are updated, as long as the quality of the spell-checker has not deteriorated. The automatic evaluation tools are available on the github repo of *divvunspell* and their integration to language development infrastructures can

[1] `https://github.com/divvun/divvunspell`

[2] `https://api-giellalt.uit.no/speller/XX`, where XX is the ISO 639 language code.

[3] the actual and up-to-date implementation of the algorithm can be found on GitHub.

be found on the actual language data repositories[4].

We experiment with a popular out-of-the-box large language model that is available for most users free of charge via a chat interface. [5] We do not perform any in-context learning or retrieval augmented generation, this is an initial experiment towards potential hybrid models of finite state and neural models of spell-checking and correction.

4 Results

We performed a small experiment to verify the working of our system and to see how well the out-of-the-box neural network works on this task. We are testing with a real-world error corpus of Finnish word-forms – 50 correctly written words and 50 spelling mistakes found in a large corpus – by picking up non-words and correcting them manually. Finnish is a morphologically complex language with medium-to-high resources. The results are in Table 1. The overall quality of both spelling checking and correction is lower in the LLM-based system than it is for the rule-based system but it still manages to provide correct suggestions almost as often as rule-based system does.

System	1st	Any
FST	70 %	88 %
LLM	50 %	85 %

Table 1: Automatic evaluation of spelling correction

5 Discussion and Future Work

We have shown a software that brings the spell-checker to end-users on mobile and desktop platforms and updates automatically when linguistic data gets developed. However, especially on mobile platforms but also increasingly on desktop, the spell-checking has been shifting towards a subfunction of a text prediction subsystem, e.g. autocomplete / autocorrect. It would be interesting future work to study possibility of such a system for morphologically complex and low-resource languages.

We only performed cursory experiments to ensure that our system works within specified parametres, the system should be functionally similar as the system evaluated by Pirinen et al. (2014) in their larger survey. We also performed the same experiment on an out-of-the-box, not fine-tuned and not prompted, re-inforced or otherwise context augmented neural network, mainly to find out their current level of quality and possible future modes of hybridisation. From the results it seems that the LLM-based systems are approaching the quality of rule-based system in terms of overall suggestions but if you concentrate on suggestion quality, it is still not comparable. More importantly, when doing a manual error evaluation, we find some examples where rule-based system is more restricted towards edit distance type error modeling, whereas LLM tends to suggest patterns of related word-forms of a same word.

One of the requirements of an end-user system in spell-checking and correction is high precision in detecting errors, the end-users tend to react very negatively of spell-checking systems that red-underline words they know are correctly written. Secondly the suggestions need to be reasonable first and foremost. Both of these aspects are relatively harder to get right with LLM solutions of today, however, there are some indications that LLMs can be more creative in error modelling, and especially when the spelling-correctors are set in the automatic text prediction context, they have been succesful. Ideally we could foresee a future system that combines the high precision of rule-based spell-checking with creative prediction of an generative AI as a potential spell-checking system.

6 Summary

We have demonstrated a spell-checking and correction system based on finite-state technology that works on end-user systems including desktop office applications and mobile phones. We tested an LLM-based approach to the same task to see where they stand at and if they could be included in the system but at the moment they are still far enough from end-user quality to be included as-is.

Limitations

The LLM test is based on one version of a closed commercial system and is not reproducible. The test is only intended to give an impression of initial usability of such systems, and for that reason we also have not included extensive descriptions of the parameters, prompts and version specifics.

[4] `https://github.com/giellalt/template-language-und`, to be refactored into `https://github.com/divvun/actions/`

[5] At the time of writing we had access to a version of ChatGPT-4o.

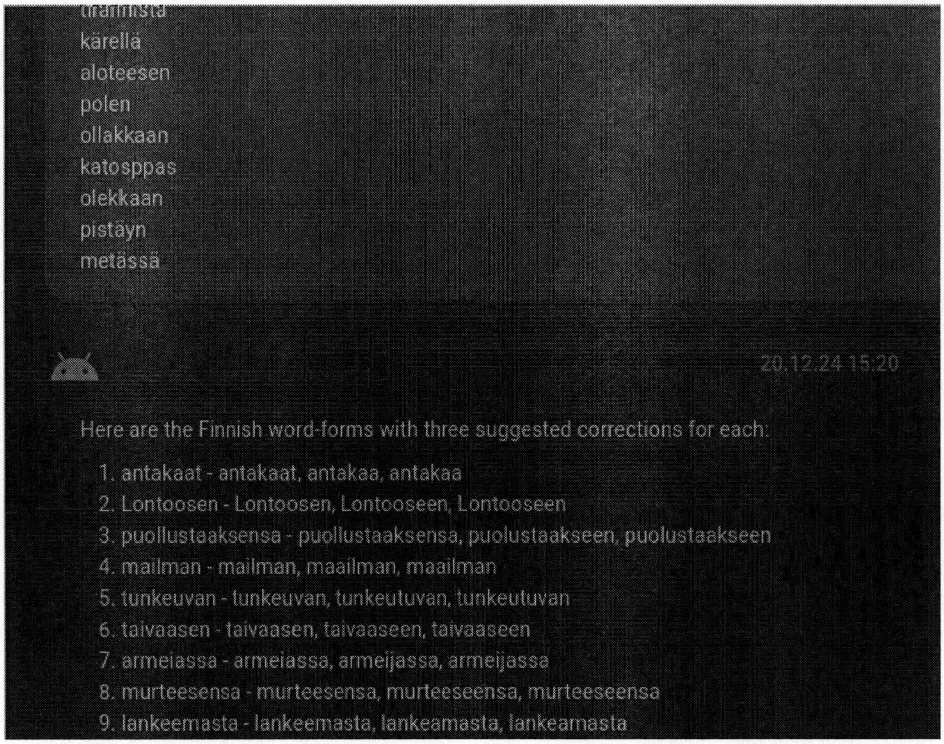

Figure 1: Example of LLM-based spell-checking and correction

```
You are a spell-checker for Finnish language,
you will be given a list of word-forms and you
should answer with a list of the word-forms,
then suggested corrections for example:
    rahhaa rahaa rahkaa
If a word is already correct,
the first suggestion should be
the same as the input word:
    päälle päälle
```

Figure 2: ChatGPT prompt for spell-checking.

The prompt used is given in the Figure 2.

Ethics Statement

The data annotation and human evaluation was performed by article authors and colleagues; no unpaid annotators were used. The LLMs use significant amount of water and electricity and we have made an effort to minimise unnecessary overuse of LLMs.

Acknowledgments

References

Kenneth R Beesley and Lauri Karttunen. 2003. *Finite State Morphology*. CSLI publications.

V. I. Levenshtein. 1966. Binary codes capable of correcting deletions, insertions, and reversals. *Soviet Physics—Doklady 10, 707–710. Translated from Doklady Akademii Nauk SSSR*, pages 845–848. Untranslated version 1965.

Peter Norvig. 2010. How to write a spelling corrector. Web page. Retrieved 2024, available `http://norvig.com/spell-correct.html`.

Flammie Pirinen, Krister Lindén, et al. 2014. State-of-the-art in weighted finite-state spell-checking. In *Computational Linguistics and Intelligent Text Processing 15th International Conference, CICLing 2014, Kathmandu, Nepal, April 6-12, 2014, Proceedings, Part II*.

Flammie Pirinen, Sjur Moshagen, and Katri Hiovain-Asikainen. 2023. GiellaLT — a stable infrastructure for Nordic minority languages and beyond. In *Proceedings of the 24th Nordic Conference on Computational Linguistics (NoDaLiDa)*, pages 643–649, Tórshavn, Faroe Islands. University of Tartu Library.

Flammie A Pirinen and Krister Lindén. 2010. Finite-state spell-checking with weighted language and error models—building and evaluating spell-checkers with wikipedia as corpus. In *7th SaLTMiL Workshop on Creation and use of basic lexical resources for less-resourced languages LREC 2010, Valetta, Malta, 23 May 2010 Workshop programme*, page 13.

Association for Computational Linguistics
209 N. Eighth Street
Stroudsburg, Pennsylvania 18360

CURRAN ASSOCIATES INC.
proceedings.com

ISBN 979-8-3313-1885-7
9 798331 318857